HYMN STORIES
FOR PROGRAMS

HYMN STORIES
FOR PROGRAMS

by

ERNEST K. EMURIAN

BAKER BOOK HOUSE
Grand Rapids, Michigan

Library of Congress Catalog Card Number: 63-22167

Copyright 1963
Baker Book House Company

ISBN: 0-8010-3274-1

Previously published under the title,
Sing the Wondrous Story

PHOTOLITHOPRINTED BY CUSHING - MALLOY, INC.
ANN ARBOR, MICHIGAN, UNITED STATES OF AMERICA
1972

When earth's noblest hymn has been written
And her final symphony scored,
When the soloist's swan-song is ended
And the organist strikes the last chord,
When the Choir's "Hallelujah" is over
And resolves to a solemn "Amen",
The creators of music, translated,
Will resume their composing again.

The faithful will sit at a console
Or wave a conductor's baton,
And bring to heroic fruition
The unfinished anthems begun;
They will have great composers to work with —
Palestrina, Beethoven and Brahms;
They will listen with awe as the angels
Sing "Masses" and "Passions" and "Psalms".

The heavens will resound with their music
And the echoes that ring from the sky
Will draw all the hearts of the nations
To the glory that dwelleth on high;
And the veil that hangs dimly between us
Will be rent as it once was of yore,
And the living, both here and hereafter,
Will join in God's praise evermore.

Ernest K. Emurian, November 10, 1962

FOREWORD

During the last few years as I have become more intimately acquainted with the authors and composers of Christendom's finest hymns and gospel songs, I have come to appreciate the varied experiences out of which so many of our sacred songs came into existence. The same God who inspired Henry van Dyke to write the stirring stanzas of "Joyful, Joyful We Adore Thee" touched the heart of Peter Bilhorn and caused him to pen the words and music of "Sweet Peace, The Gift Of God's Love" just as He touched the British barrister Frederic Weatherly who gave us the thrilling imagery of "The Holy City" as well as the sentimental verses of "Danny Boy". Likewise, the Philadelphian who authored and composed "Whispering Hope" and then published it under a female pseudonym, was the same musician and poet who fathered "Listen To The Mocking Bird". In like manner, I have also become aware of the fact that Christianity alone of all the religions of the world has inspired women to sing and then has accepted their stanzas and placed them alongside those of men in the hymnals of the faith, an eloquent tribute to the elevating and equalizing power of Jesus Christ. So I have included the stories of Eliza E. Hewitt and Lelia Naylor Morris along with those of William Pierson Merrill and Thomas Tiplady, for God certainly sang as musically if not as brilliantly through feminine as through masculine hearts. If the reading of these chapters awakens in the hearts and minds of those who appreciate Christianity's noble heritage of hymnody and sacred song the realization that "God did not stop singing when David died" and causes them to drink more deeply from the springs which the pioneering creators of yesterday and today have tapped, the author's labors will have been worthwhile.

ERNEST K. EMURIAN
Cherrydale Methodist Church
Arlington, Virginia

CONTENTS

1.

MALTBIE DAVENPORT BABCOCK

This Is My Father's World   Be Strong

Maltbie Davenport Babcock (1858-1901) was such a remarkable and talented Presbyterian clergyman that a colleague spoke
of him as "an honored and beloved brother who possessed the
sweet singing soul of David, the fiery zeal of Apostle Paul, the
eloquence of Apollos, the capacity for friendship of Jonathan and
the heavenly spirit of St. John", a tribute with which the pastor's
devoted parishioners heartily concurred, both in his initial pastorate in Lockport, New York (1882-1887) as well as in his subsequent successful pastorates at the Brown Memorial Church,
Baltimore (1887-1899) and in the Brick Church of New York
City (1900-1901). Whether he actually did possess that rare and
remarkable combination of "heavenly attributes" or not, it would
have taken a man of all that and more to acceptably fill the prominent pulpits that were his during his all-too-brief active ministry
of less than twenty years.

A native of Syracuse, New York, where he was born on August
3, 1858, the gifted preacher-to-be entered the University in his
own city after completing his high school education, graduating
in 1879, his twenty-first year. He received his theological training at Auburn Seminary and was then ordained as a Presbyterian
minister soon after receiving his Bachelor of Divinity degree in
1882, assuming the responsibilities of leading the Presbyterian
congregation in nearby Lockport that same summer. Nearly three
months after he was installed in his first pastorate, Babcock and
Miss Katherine Tallman were united in marriage, the date of
their wedding being October 4, 1882.

A man full of fun and glowing with an unusual and radiant
inner "holy joy", he had quite early distinguished himself not

only as a student and scholar but also as a musician and student leader, excelling in dramatics as well as athletics and finding time for nature study as well as religious activity. His profound personal faith in God and in the beneficent workings of His Divine Providence, coupled with his genuine optimism and magnetic personality, drew men to him and held them at his side with a loyalty and love that could never be demanded but only freely and willingly bestowed. In his later, more mature years, his reputation as a college champion in baseball and swimming preceded him and inspired many a curious student to grant him a hearing as he spoke on many campuses throughout the East, as a result of which many came to view the Christian life in a fresh light and gave to Babcock's Christ their own personal allegiance.

During his years in Lockport, he would frequently don some old clothes early in the morning and jog up a nearby hill to view the beauties of "his Father's world" as they unfolded before him in a sweeping panorama that had as its backdrop the waters of Lake Ontario on the distant horizon. "This world is the best for us," he was often heard to say, "and we must·make the most of it and do our best for it.". Some of his dawn and dusk hikes took him to a distant forest grove, where he enjoyed bird-watching, counting sometimes as many as forty different varieties of birds simultaneously lifting their tiny chirping voices in songs of praise to their Creator. This time of communion saw nature working her therapeutic miracle of healing not only on the busy minister's body, but also on his mind and soul, better preparing him to serve his people in the wide variety of ways demanded of a sincere servant of Jesus Christ.

It came as no surprise to his people, then, when their preacher turned poet and reduced his observations and convictions to a series of couplets, each one of which began with the bold affirmation, forged on the anvil of his own experience, "This is my Father's world," containing, among others, these colorful and descriptive lines:

1. "This is my Father's world, And to my listening ears
   All nature sings and round me rings The music of the spheres.
2. This is my Father's world. I rest me in the thought

Of rocks and trees, of skies and seas, His hand the wonders
wrought.

3. This is my Father's world. The birds their carols raise;
The morning light, the lily white, Declare their Maker's
praise.

4. This is my Father's world. He shines in all that's fair.
In the rustling grass I hear Him pass, He speaks to me
everywhere.

5. This is my Father's world. O let me ne'er forget
That though the wrong seems oft so strong, God is the
ruler yet.

6. This is my Father's world. Why should my heart be sad?
The Lord is King — let the Heavens ring, God reigns —
let the earth be glad."

When an urgent call from the Brown Memorial Presbyterian
Church of Baltimore reached him, young Babcock, not yet thirty
years of age, felt that it was God's will, so he resigned from his
Lockport Church and moved to the Maryland city little dreaming
that he was soon to become the city's most popular preacher and
most sought-after counsellor, advisor, comforter and friend. His
contagiously radiant personality drew the students and faculty
members of Johns Hopkins University to his Church in larger
and larger numbers, while many of them came to know him personally, drawing spiritual strength from the deep wells of his own
religious fervor and faith. It was during these busy and crowded
years (1887-1899) that Babcock penned a simple four-line poem
that revealed the secret of his own dynamic Christian life:

"Back of the loaf is the snowy flour, Back of the flour the mill;
Back of the mill is the wheat and the shower, The sun and the
Father's will."

Invitations to preach to many University audiences poured in
to the busy pastor's desk, and he accepted as many as time and
strength allowed, influencing the lives of thousands of students
by means of this expanding campus ministry. When the distinguished Presbyterian clergyman, poet, preacher, author, and
statesman, Henry van Dyke, relinquished his post at the Brick
Church in New York City, the popular Baltimore pastor was
invited to move once more and assume the duties and responsi-

11

bilities of serving one of the most influential Presbyterian congregations in the nation's largest metropolis, an invitation he was unable to decline. One of his most ardent admirers said of his acceptance, "As surely as Paul was called to Mars Hill, Babcock was called to Murray Hill", since the Church at the dawn of the twentieth century was located at Fifth Avenue and Thirty-Seventh Street in the Murray Hill section of the city. Of his brief ministry there, his predecessor later wrote "he preached the Word with gladness, comforted the sorrowful with tender mercy and brought a blessing in the name of Christ to the hearts of his people who remember him ever with grateful love."

Again more and more people crowded the Church sanctuary on Sunday morning, to the consternation of the ushers who found it well nigh impossible to keep hundreds of "strangers" from occupying the pews reserved for regular members who paid an annual rent for the privilege of being guaranteed a seat at every service. And here the many demands of a metropolitan pulpit bore heavily upon the heart and shoulders of the stalwart spiritual giant, giving him less time than ever before to get "out in the fields with God" and to rest and recuperate among the beauties of his "Father's world". While his people were saying that "his life itself is a hymn of praise", Babcock was carrying burdensome loads, and finding little time "to play, to dream, to drift".

Out of this trying period in his life the preacher-poet penned a poem that seemed to some of his intimate friends to be more autobiographical than any he had previously written, for in it he hurled a challenge and revealed an inner conflict between the work he felt compelled to do and the strength he knew was unequal to the task. Drawing inspiration from Ephesians 6:10, in which Paul had written "Be strong in the Lord and in the power of his might", and from 2 Timothy 2:1, in which the older Apostle had advised his young ministerial protege to "Be strong in the grace that is in Christ Jesus", Babcock, now reaching the zenith of his powers as preacher and pastor, wrote:

1. "Be strong! We are not here to play, to dream, to drift;
   We have hard work to do and loads to lift.
   Shun not the struggle. Face it! 'Tis God's gift. Be Strong!
2. Be strong! Say not the days are evil. Who's to blame?

12

And fold your hands and acquiesce. O Shame!
Stand up, speak out and bravely, in God's Name. Be
    Strong!
3. Be strong! It matters not how deep entrenched the wrong.
    How hard the battle goes; the day how long!
    Faint not, fight on, tomorrow comes the song! Be strong!"

His shepherd heart led him to visit every home in his parish during the first twelve months of his New York ministry, a period in the congregation's life later referred to as "The Golden Year".

After a memorable and enviable record in a new field of service, the forty-three year old pastor planned an extended trip to Egypt and Palestine, his people gladly giving him all the time necessary to make his first trip overseas a completely satisfying experience. He preached his last sermon at the Brick Church on February 24, 1901 to such a large crowd that one reporter present wrote, "The ushers will undoubtedly be pleased once their pastor is safely on his way to Egypt." Thus with a pastorate of less than a year and a half behind him, the pastor and a group of friends sailed from New York for the Mediterranean, his keen observations and reflections being regularly reported to his people back home in a series of communications which he entitled "Letters from Egypt and Palestine". His sight-seeing behind him, and the journey home being welcomed with as much anticipation as had his departure a few months earlier, Babcock and his companions began the long voyage back to the United States, a trip the brilliant preacher was never to complete. Contracting a strange and rather mysterious eastern fever, he was taken from his ship in Naples, Italy, and placed in the International Hospital there early in May of that same year, dying a few days later, on May 18, 1901 in the forty-third year of his earthly pilgrimage. His body was taken to Syracuse for final services and burial.

His wife who outlived him by more than two-score years, gathered up her husband's finest prose and poetic writings, publishing them six months after his untimely death in a volume entitled "Thoughts For Every Day Living", in which publication the stanzas of his two best poems were offered to the public for the first time. Although the poet-preacher little realized that his stanzas had hymnic possibilities, from that volume they eventually

13

found their way into the hymnals of Christendom. While one of his ardent admirers spoke of Babcock as "a well-born, athletic person, who was a fine musician, a clever poet with the instincts of an artist, a clear thinker, a powerful and persuasive orator with that certain indefinable personal magnetism which gave him power over an individual in conversation or an audience in preaching", and another added that his poems revealed "a touch of Emerson, a touch of Browning and a touch of his favorite, Wordsworth", he did what most of these men were unable to do. Unknowingly, and yet effectively and providentially he enriched the hymnody of his day, leaving as his finest legacy two of the most inspiring and yet most contrasting hymns of the twentieth century.

2.

WILLIAM PIERSON MERRILL

Not Alone For Mighty Empire   Rise Up, O Men Of God

Rarely has the pulpit committee of any leading Protestant Church shown the consistently good judgment in the selection of its ministers as has that of New York City's Brick (Presbyterian) Church. Several of the Church's most prominent pastors have not only been "pulpit giants" but also prolific poets and hymn-writers of unusual talent. Rev. Henry Van Dyke, who was the shepherd of that congregation from 1883 until 1900, was the author of the hymn "Joyful Joyful We Adore Thee" which is sung universally to Edward Hodges' arrangement of the theme from The Choral (last) Movement of Beethoven's Ninth Symphony. His immediate successor, Rev. Maltbie Davenport Babcock, whose brief ministry during 1900 and 1901 was terminated by his untimely death at the age of forty-three, authored such poetic masterpieces as "This Is My Father's World" and "Be Strong". The last of the trio of pastor-poets was Rev. William Pierson Merrill, who served that same congregation the longest tenure of them all, ministering there for twenty-seven years, from 1911 until he was made pastor emeritus in 1938. Merrill, a native of Orange, New Jersey, where he was born in 1867, took his college training at Rutgers and his seminary studies at New York City's Union Theological Seminary, accepting a call from Trinity Church, Chestnut Hill, Philadelphia soon after receiving his Bachelor of Divinity degree. After five years in the City of Brotherly Love, he assumed the pastoral oversight of Chicago's Sixth Presbyterian Church, filling its pulpit with distinction for sixteen years, from 1895 until 1911, when he accepted an urgent invitation to return to New York City as pastor of the Brick Church, where he labored untiringly and with notable success for more than a quarter of a century. It was during the closing year of his Chicago pastorate that the busy pastor, browsing through the pages of a popular religious journal, came across an article entitled, "The Church of The Strong Men", from the pen of Gerald Stanley Lee. Since the Windy City clergyman had already gained quite a reputation for himself as a "battler for unpopular righteous causes", and was well aware of the duties that true Christian devotion demanded of every person who "took up his cross" to follow Christ, the caption of Lee's article fired his imagination. No doubt, as he quickly read what the other man had written, he recalled some lines from Tennyson's "In Memoriam" (1849), in which the brilliant British Poet-Laureate had spoken of The Master as "Strong Son of God, Immortal Love", although Lee's plea was for more "strong men" to follow such a "strong leader". Even though Merrill did not know at that particular time that the New York pulpit would be offered to him the following year, a former pastor of that congregation, Maltbie Babcock (1858-1901), had written his hymn "Be Strong" some years earlier, but it had not been published until 1902, several months after his tragic death in Naples, Italy, on his way home from an extended trip to Egypt and the Holy Land.

Merrill could not get Lee's title or article out of his mind and heart, and they remained there in a state of intellectual incubation until he was approached by a fellow Chicagoan, Nolan R. Best, who was then editing a local Presbyterian magazine "The Continent", with an unusual request. Best and the dynamic clergyman were already fast friends, and had already collaborated on other matters of mutual interest, the editor at one time writing some stanzas entitled "Made Of One Blood With All The Earth" for which the preacher had composed an original hymn tune. But this time, his fellow-Presbyterian urged his colleague to try his hand at writing the stanzas of a stirring new hymn on the all-inclusive theme of Christian Brotherhood, in keeping with the Brotherhood movement that was sweeping through the Presbyterian congregations of the United States.

Although Merrill later confessed that the steps leading up to the actual writing of his finest hymn were "simple and uninteresting", those who have been inspired by the singing of his inspired lines can justifiably disagree. Many divergent forces at work in different places finally converged in what was to be Merrill's hymnic masterpiece.

Best knew what he was doing when he pressed the matter upon the other man's heart, however, and he felt his request was well within the bounds of reason and propriety, for he had already printed in the columns of "The Continent" that very same year several stanzas from his comrade's pen which revealed the poetic soul of the pastor-preacher, and he deemed it not inappropriate to encourage him to "do it again" while the "artistic muse" was still hovering about his brilliant mind and putting a creative cutting edge upon his fertile imagination.

The Chicago divine's previous poem had contained these significant "Thanksgiving" lines:

1. "Not alone for mighty empire, Stretching far O'er land and sea;
   Not alone for bounteous harvests, Lift we up our hearts to Thee.
   Standing in the living present, Memory and hope between,
   Lord we would with deep thanksgiving Praise Thee most for things unseen.

2. Not for battleship and fortress, Not for conquests of the sword;
   But for conquests of the spirit Give we thanks to Thee, O Lord;
   For the priceless gift of freedom, For the home, the church, the school;
   For the open door to manhood In a land the people rule.

3. For the armies of the faithful, Souls that passed and left no name;
   For the glory that illumines Patriot lives of deathless fame;
   For our prophets and apostles, Loyal to the living Word;
   For all heroes of the Spirit, Give we thanks to Thee, O Lord.

4. God of justice, save the people From the clash of race and creed,

From the strife of class and faction: Make our nation free
indeed.
Keep her faith in simple manhood Strong as when her life
began,
Till it finds its full fruition In the brotherhood of man."

As the preacher distilled the meat of Lee's article once more against the background of Best's suggestion about a new hymn, he immediately and almost unconsciously concluded that a Church of strong men would be a Church thoroughly alive with men who would be willing to rise up and follow Christ as their Lord and Master at whatever cost. "Lazy men keep their seats while strong men are unafraid to stand up and be counted," he must have thought. Steeped in Christian hymnody as well as in her theology, he recalled the oft-sung lines of John Greenleaf Whittier's hymn "Dear Lord And Father Of Mankind" in which the Quaker poet had written, in 1872, this concluding exhortation: "Let us, like them (the disciples), without a word, Rise up and follow Thee." Being familiar with the life and teachings of Jesus, Merrill soon recalled the command of the Lord to the impotent man at the pool of Bethesda whom He healed on the Sabbath day with the simple but stern admonition, "Rise, take up thy bed and walk" (John 5:8), as well as His words to the paralytic whose four friends had brought him to the Master for healing, "Rise up and walk" (Luke 5:23) and to the man whose withered hand He cured on a subsequent Sabbath, His command, "Rise up and stand forth in the midst" (Luke 6:8). All of these thoughts gradually matured in the minister's mind finally, and rather unexectedly, bearing fruit a hundred-fold as he was aboard a steamer crossing Lake Michigan in order to fill a Sunday appointment in his Chicago pulpit. Quite likely, his absence from the pressing and perplexing duties of his big city parish enabled him to view his ministry from a fresh perspective, and evaluate it anew in the light of the complete gospel that Jesus had proclaimed centuries ago. Also, his own relaxation of body and mind during the long boat trip brought with it a certain mental clarity and sharpness that were just what he needed in order to do his best creative work. Without too much actual conscious effort on the

18

preacher's part, the stanzas that had eluded him so long suddenly seemed to rise almost effortlessly from the overflow of his conse-crated heart and dedicated, disciplined mind. Soon he found him-self writing down several stanzas in a poetic meter he readily recognized as Short Meter, (four-line poems, with the first, second and fourth lines having six syllables, while the third line had eight). In a rhyming rhythmic spirit, he was jotting down this exhortation:

1. "Rise up, O men of God! Have done with lesser things;
   Give heart and mind and soul and strength To serve the King of Kings.

2. Rise up, O men of God! His kingdom tarries long;
   Bring in the day of brotherhood And end the night of wrong.

3. Rise up, O men of God! The Church for you doth wait;
   Her strength unequal to her task; Rise up and make her great!

4. Lift high the cross of Christ! Tread where His feet have trod;
   As brothers of the Son of man, Rise up, O men of God!"

Seventeen years prior to that memorable creative hour in the life of the Chicago Presbyterian clergyman, a composer named William H. Walter (1825-1893) had composed a new tune for a hymn by William Hammond, which was entitled "Awake And Sing The Song", a piece of music the composer fittingly named "Festal Song". When Merrill's thrilling stanzas were included in "The Pilgrim Hymnal" of 1912, within a year after they had been written, they were wedded to Walter's stirring tune, and from the pages of that publication the words and music have gone into the hymnals of the Church universal. Although some editors favored other melodies, the familiar dynamic message and earnest exhortation of the preacher-poet's stanzas remained constant through the years. When the Father of American Hymnology and Public School Music, Dr. Lowell Mason (1792-1872), discovered Ray Palmer's beautiful devotional poem "My Faith Looks Up To Thee", he not only set it to music, but also prophesied that long after the poet had "finished his course" and regardless of the great accomplishments that might attend his ministry, future generations would remember him for the four simple autobiographical stanzas he had penned one afternoon during his twenty-second year. The fact that Mason's prophecy came true makes another such utterance all the more significant, for the famous American preacher, Rev. S. Parks Cadman, one of the pulpit giants of American Protestantism, made similar remarks about his brother minister, Rev. William Pierson Merrill and his moving hymn "Rise Up, O Men Of God", words that the passing of time seems to be authenticating in a remarkable way. The close of that same year, 1911, saw Merrill moving to New York City to begin another distinguished pastorate that was to see his influence as a preacher, pastor, poet and pioneer extend far beyond the narrow confines of his own Presbyterian parish and even beyond the boundaries of his own city, state and denomination. Although he wrote many books and successfully championed many worthwhile causes during his long and active ministry, when Dr. Merrill died in New York City on June 20, 1954, at the age of eighty-seven, his obituaries spoke of him as a "minister, author and hymn-writer" but the greatest of these was "hymn-writer".

3.

HENRY VAN DYKE

Joyful, Joyful We Adore Thee

The eminent Scottish Presbyterian divine, Rev. George Matheson (1842-1906), had several things in common with the prominent American Presbyterian clergyman, Rev. Henry Van Dyke (1852-1933), among them being their ability to inspire great multitudes from the pulpit with an English style that was revealing and captivating at the same time, and the poetic gift that enabled each man to contribute to the hymnology of his own day and thereby enrich the hymnody of Christendom for future generations. Matheson, the blind pulpiteer whose magnificent and deeply spiritual sermons attracted great congregations to his Edinburgh pastorate, wrote some of the most beautiful sacred prose of the nineteenth century, in addition to penning such poetic masterpieces as "O Love That Wilt Not Let Me Go" and "Make Me A Captive, Lord". Van Dyke, on the other hand, gained renown not only as a professor and preacher but also as an author, poet and political statesman, in addition to earning an enviable reputation as a platform speaker and lecturer.

A native of Germantown, Pennsylvania, where he was born November 10, 1852, Henry took his graduate and post-graduate degrees from Brooklyn Tech and Princeton, receiving his Bachelor of Arts in 1873, at twenty-one, and his Master's Degree three years later, in 1876, just six years before Matheson wrote his great autobiographical hymn on the other side of the Atlantic Ocean. Van Dyke continued his studies at Princeton Theological Seminary over on the hill just a block or two from the University campus, and, upon completing his "days of preparation", entered upon his first pastorate at the Union Congregational Church in Newport, Rhode Island, although he had been ordained a Presbyterian.

21

He reached the height of his influence and the zenith of his pulpit powers within the next two decades, his talents being recognized when he was called to the influential pulpit of the Brick Presbyterian Church in the Murray Hill section of New York City in 1883, a pastorate he relinquished seventeen years later to another preacher-poet, Rev. Maltbie Davenport Babcock (1858-1901). Van Dyke's remarkable pulpit style as well as the consistently constructive content of his sermons drew larger and larger congregations to Murray Hill, while his unusual command of the English language made publishers vie for the privilege of "signing him up on the dotted line" so they could make his written works available to an eager public.

It came as no surprise, then, when his writings attracted as much favorable comment as the sermons he delivered from his pulpit Sunday after Sunday. When his Alma Mater, Princeton University, extended him an invitation to return to the New Jersey campus as Professor of English Literature, no one was unduly surprised when Van Dyke enthusiastically accepted. For the next two decades the renowned pastor-preacher-poet filled his new position with rare distinction.

The breadth of his understanding and sympathy is nowhere more evident than in his offer to correct what he considered a "serious defect" in the stanzas of one of his country's most popular patriotic hymns, "America", written in 1832 by another clergyman-to-be, Baptist-born Rev. Samuel Francis Smith (1808-1895). Considering the four stanzas of his fellow-countryman a bit "too New-Englandish" in character to be acceptable to the newer states of the expanding Republic, the Princeton professor dared to add some lines of his own to Smith's original, stanzas he felt would include some of the distinctive characteristics of the southern and western states which he found lacking in the older man's verses. Although they never supplanted the originals in the hearts and minds of the American people, nevertheless, Van Dyke offered these additional stanzas to the growing population of his native land in his one-man effort to bring "America" "up to date";

1. I love thine inland seas, Thy groves of giant trees, Thy rolling plains;

Thy mighty rivers' sweep; Majestic canyons deep; Thy
mountains wild and steep,
All Thy domains.
2. Thy silver eastern strand, Thy Golden Gate that stands
Fronting the west;
Thy flowing southland fair, Thy sweet and crystal air — O
land beyond compare,
Thee I love best.

During his Princeton years, the Presbyterian clergyman developed a fast friendship with one of his Alma Mater's most distinguished presidents, Woodrow Wilson. Their mutual admiration
and esteem, recognized readily by students and faculty members
alike, was revealed to the nation at large when Wilson, as President of the United States, appointed his Princeton colleague to the
post of United States Minister to Holland and Luxemburg when
that position became available in 1913, Van Dyke serving his
country overseas until the outbreak of hostilities in 1917. By
that time his popularity and influence had increased beyond his
imagining, principally by means of one of his books, "The Other
Wise Man", which, although first published in 1896, was well
on its way to becoming an American classic, a literary position
the volume still enjoys more than half a century after its initial
publication.

Twenty-eight years prior to Van Dyke's birth in the United
States, a fifty-four year old composer, Ludwig Beethoven, conducted a symphony orchestra and chorus in Austria's capital city
Vienna in the premier performance of his majestic Ninth Symphony, a composition rarely equalled and never surpassed in the
history of instrumental and choral music. Ironically, the composer
was so deaf that he was unable to hear the resounding applause
with which the Viennese people heralded their most renowned
citizen's greatest work that February night in 1824, and a member
of the orchestra had to take the master by the shoulders and
turn him around before he knew that his Ninth, and last, Symphony had been accepted by those for whom he had created it.
Seldom has any composer received such a well-merited ovation
as the audience gave Beethoven that memorable night.

When the German-born musician and composer first conceived

his last symphonic work, it was as an instrumental composition only, in the style of his eight earlier symphonies, but when he began writing down the notes of the fourth and final movement, the thrilling words of Schiller's "Ode To Joy" inspired him to such a degree that he felt that only the addition of human voices to the orchestral score could express the music he heard within his heart and give full fervor to the themes that kept dancing through his fertile brain. Johann Cristoph Friedrich von Schiller (1759-1805) had been in his grave less than twenty years when Beethoven suddenly remembered the moving and majestic lines of one of his fellow-German's most joyous lyrics and determined to give them a prominent and permanent place in the final movement of what was destined to be his last and greatest symphony.

In Vienna, professional guides remind the tourist that Beethoven composed his Eroica Symphony while living at #92 Doblinger Hauptstrasse, and his Pastorale Symphony while residing at #26 Kahlenbergerstrasse, and at #64 Grinzingerstrasse, while the house at #18 Molkerbastei is pointed out as the official Beethoven museum in the city, although the composer had lived in many different sections of the Austrian capital during the years 1804-1815. It was while he made his home at #5 Ungargasse that he composed and perfected his monumental Ninth Symphony. At the time of his death in 1827, Beethoven was living at #15 Schwarzpanierstrasse, while his monument stands in what has been renamed the Beethovenplatz in his honor.

Born in Bonn, Germany, in 1770, Beethoven always regarded his meeting with Franz Joseph Haydn in 1792 as the turning point in his career, this encounter providing the spark that inspired him to compose 138 numbered works as well as more than 70 unnumbered compositions, among them nine of the world's noblest symphonies, in addition to many of music's most superbly organized piano sonatas and orchestral compositions for smaller instrumental groups. A man whose life was characterized by "genius, generosity and geniality", the composer's last years were haunted by increasing personal deafness and added heartbreak brought about by the scandalous behaviour of an ungrateful nephew whom he had befriended. But none of that is evident in the joyous strains which permeate the choral movement of the symphony, revealing that the composer drew strength from deeper wells and built his musical superstructure on surer foundations.

It remained for a British-born organist to adapt the musical theme of Beethoven's orchestral and vocal "swan song" for hymnic purposes, and when Edward Hodges (1796-1867) performed his labor of love he little dreamed that it would occasion Henry Van Dyke's most inspired paean of praise. Although he left his native country long enough to serve three "foreign" appointments overseas, one stint in Toronto, Canada and two in New York City, where he served successively as organist at St. John's Episcopal Church and Trinity Church, Hodges left as his finest legacy a four-part arrangement of Beethoven's grandest theme which made it possible for the music to be used as a hymn tune for services of public worship in Churches of Christian nations on both sides of the Atlantic.

Although many poets had attempted to express in the English language the lofty sentiments of Schiller's joyous Ode which Beethoven mastered so effectively in his musical score, most of their efforts had been ignored or just politely forgotten as unworthy of the music whose spirit they had failed to capture in words. Van Dyke was quickly conscious of the fact that a fitting poem had to be as much an original work as a translation, yet expressive of all lands and times and at the same time overflowing with such a radiant spirit that it would harmonize with Hodges' arrangement in such a manner that "martial joy would mature into true religious ecstacy". During one of his visits to the campus of Williams College, the preacher-professor-politician set himself to the task of penning appropriate stanzas in the 8.7.8.7.D meter which had characterized Schiller's original, the eight lines of every stanza containing alternately eight and seven syllables each. That he succeeded is attested by the fact that his four stanzas are now found in practically every Hymnal of every leading Protestant denomination in the English-singing world. In his descriptive lines, the poet revealed the depth of his own stalwart Christian faith as well as the breadth of his Christian outreach and love. Among his best lines were these:

1. "Joyful, joyful, we adore Thee, God of glory, Lord of love;

Hearts unfold like flow'rs before Thee, Opening to the sun above.

Melt the clouds of sin and sadness, Drive the dark of doubt away;

Giver of immortal gladness, Fill us with the light of day!"

2. "All Thy works with joy surround Thee, Earth and heaven reflect Thy rays,

   Stars and angels sing around Thee, Center of unbroken praise;

   Field and forest, vale and mountain, Flowery meadow, flashing sea,

   Chanting bird and flowing fountain, Call us to rejoice in Thee."

3. "Thou art giving and forgiving, Ever blessing, ever blest,

   Well-spring of the joy of living, Ocean-depth of happy rest!

   Thou our Father, Christ our Brother — All who live in love are Thine;

   Teach us how to love each other, Lift us to the Joy Divine."

4. "Mortals join the mighty chorus, Which the morning stars began;

   Father-love is reigning o'er us, Brother-love binds man to man.

   Ever singing, march we onward, Victors in the midst of strife;

   Joyful music leads us sunward, In the triumph-song of life."

Over forty books came from Van Dyke's fluent pen, while other original hymns on a wide variety of subjects enriched the hymnody of his own day. Despite the numerous honors that were heaped in profusion upon him in his older years, he continued to devote himself to his literary pursuits in his Princeton residence, while following his hobbies as an ardent outdoorsman and fisherman as often as he found the time. Thus from the most majestic composition of a German composer arranged by a Britisher who did his best work in America, coupled with a poem by a native American Presbyterian clergyman, this glorious hymn came into existence. The passing of the years only finds it growing in favor, its insistent note of "holy joy" and its constant exhortation to "holy love" making it one of the "poetic pearls" of the current century.

4.

EARL MARLATT

Are Ye Able?

Of the many requests made of Jesus during the three years of His earthly ministry, none was more unusual, more shocking or more demanding than that made of Him by Salome, the mother of two of His Apostles, James and John, the sons of Zebedee. As recorded in Matthew 20:20-28, when Jesus and His band of followers were enroute to Jerusalem, Salome asked a certain favor of the Lord, saying unto Him, "Grant that these my two sons may sit, the one at thy right and the other at thy left in thy kingdom."

Jesus well knew what the devoted mother had in mind for oriental potentates always rewarded their closest friends and boon companions by permitting them to occupy the second and third highest offices in the land, symbolized by having seats on the right and left of the ruler's throne. Instead of rebuking her for this strange request on behalf of the brothers He had nicknamed "The Sons Of Thunder" Jesus in turn asked James and John a question. "Are ye able to drink of the cup that I shall drink of, and to be baptized with the baptism that I am baptized with?" He asked them, signifying the sufferings He was soon to undergo as well as the cruel death He was soon to die. Undaunted, they replied "We are able."

Sensing their over-confidence, Jesus continued, "Ye shall drink indeed of my cup and be baptized with the baptism that I am baptized with; but to sit on my right hand and on my left is not mine to give, but it shall be given to them for whom it is prepared of my Father."

This incident has inspired many a sermon and many a classroom lecture in many a theological seminary, and, through the ages, has been used by preachers and teachers alike to hold before their hearers the challenges of the Christian life. Among those who used it with telling effect was a teacher at Boston University School of Theology, Marcus D. Buell, and among those who sat at his feet and never forgot the dramatic intensity with which the professor pictured James and John replying, "We are able", was a theology student by the name of Earl Bowman Marlatt. Years later young Marlatt recalled almost the exact words with which his teacher had made that Biblical incident come to life after the passing of nearly two thousand years, and he remembered that Buell had said, "Jesus knew that just ahead of Him was Jerusalem and possibly crucifixion and He wondered if the young men had courage enough to follow Him that far." In that spirit He had asked His question and in a moment of high enthusiasm and remarkable boldness, they had made their startling reply.

Marlatt, one of twin sons born into a Methodist minister's home in Columbus, Indiana in May, 1892, had entered the Seminary after graduating from De Pauw University, studying theology from 1919 until 1922. Two years after receiving his degree he travelled throughout Europe, visiting among other notable places, the mountain village of Oberammergau, where, with thousands of other travellers and tourists, he saw the world-famous Passion Play. The scene from this thrilling drama that impressed him above all others was that in which the penitent thief cried out for forgiveness and heard the Master's words, "Today thou shalt be with me in paradise." Marlatt continued his studies at Oxford in England and at the University of Berlin in Germany, entering the United States Army during the First World War, and serving as a second lieutenant in the field artillery. He accepted the position as an associate professor of Philosophy in Boston University in 1923, becoming a full professor two years later, in 1925. It was in 1926, the year after his election to a full professorship in his Alma Mater, that these two experiences of previous years merged into one when he was asked to write an original hymn for a Consecration Service for the Theological Seminary's School of Religious Education, of which he was then also a faculty member. A graduate student at the seminary, Henry Silvermale Mason, had composed an original tune two years earlier, in 1924, a piece of music he had played so often for his fellow classmates and others that all of them knew it by heart. When thirty-four year old Professor Marlatt thought about forty-three year old Mason's two-year old hymn tune, and linked it in his mind with the words of his professor Marcus Buell, and the thrill of the Passion Play which he never forgot, the pieces of the hymnic puzzle seemed to fall almost automatically and quite spontaneously into place.

As the young teacher walked across historic Boston Common that afternoon in 1926, things "clicked" with remarkable precision, and before he reached his room on Boston's Beacon Hill that evening, his hymn was practically complete. All he needed now was to write down his stanzas and the words for the Chorus, and submit them to the quartet and congregation for their approval or disapproval. Three days later, "Are Ye Able" was sung publicly for the first time in Pilgrim Hall at the scheduled Service of Consecration, the new hymn of self-dedication meeting with an instantaneously favorable response. In his opening stanza, the poet-preacher had taken the words of Jesus directly out of the Authorized Version (1611) of the Holy Bible and had asked,
"Are ye able," said the Master, "To be crucified with Me?"
"Yea," the sturdy dreamers answered, "To the death we follow Thee."
With the incident from the Passion Play clearly before him, he versified the cry of the dying thief in the second stanza, while his third dealt with the assurance of immortality which is every Christian's prized possession. His fourth and last stanza still began with the same three words "Are ye able" but pictured the Master as asking that same question of every believer of every age as He had asked it first of James and John, concluding that "heroic spirits" today answer as positively as did those disciples of yore, since His "guiding radiance" would ever be for all of them and us, "A beacon to God, to love and loyalty".

When this new hymn began to be used at subsequent consecration services sponsored by other branches of the Seminary and University, its future was assured and its adoption as one of the official songs of the school of theology and the university was almost an anti-climax. Significantly, the tune Mason had composed two years before Marlatt penned his moving lines, was named "Beacon Hill". And, interestingly enough, both the composer and the poet dedicated their different talents to the training of students for the Christian ministry, Marlatt serving his Alma Mater with distinction and then assuming similar responsibilities at the Perkins School of Theology at Southern Methodist University in Texas, while Mason did his teaching at the Auburn Theological Seminary at Auburn, New York.

Seldom has a hymn spread so rapidly or caught on so quickly, but the students of these teachers picked it up and carried it to the four corners of Christendom, where its challenging cry reminded other generations of preachers and laymen of the price James and John had paid for their devotion to Jesus, and the demands and duties which He lays upon the disciples of every century, until, in His service, they are transformed into the delights of His modern-day disciples, as they sing together,
"Lord, we are able, Our spirits are Thine;
Remould them, make us Like Thee divine.
Thy guiding radiance above us shall be
A beacon to God, to love and loyalty."

Although he has written many splendid hymns and sacred poems, Dr. Marlatt, who earned his Doctor of Philosophy degree but was awarded an honorary Doctor of Letters by his Alma Mater, penned his second best known hymn when a student in one of his Church History classes queried him about the meaning of the Holy Trinity. In jest, he told the inquirer that he would sing it in poetry rather than attempt to explain it in prose. Out of that experience, Marlatt wrote the five stanzas of his hymn "Spirit Of Life" which began with these lines,
"Spirit of Life, in this new dawn, Give us the faith that follows on,
Letting Thine all-pervading power Fulfill the dream of this high hour."

Subsequent stanzas addressed the third Person of the Trinity as "Spirit Creative, Redeeming, Consoling and Spirit of Love". It is significant that both of his finest hymns may be linked together since their basic messages are one, for only those who are filled with God's Spirit are inspired and empowered to say, "We are able".

5.

P. P. BLISS

Almost Persuaded
Wonderful Words Of Life   I Will Sing Of My Redeemer

Philip Paul Bliss and Abraham Lincoln had this one thing in common: both were born in log cabins. Bliss, the son of a musical and deeply religious father, was born in the northern Pennsylvania county of Clearfield on July 9, 1838. He was ten years old when he heard a piano for the first time. The music so entranced the barefoot youngster that he said to the young lady when she stopped, "O lady, play some more." Although she rebuked him for his boldness, she did not destroy his love of music. The famous composer, George F. Root, became one of his teachers. Later, Mr. William Bradbury, another famous composer, encouraged Bliss to establish himself as a music teacher, which he finally agreed to do about the year 1860, when he was just twenty-two. Four years later he wrote and sold his first original composition to the Chicago publishing firm of Root and Cady, a ballad "Lora Vale", which became an immediate musical success. Little did he dream, then, that God had marked him for more serious work and had already set him apart for composing music of a more lasting nature.

As for his religious life, Bliss was about as ecumenical a composer as the nineteenth century afforded. At twelve he was immersed into the Cherry Flats Baptist Church, Tioga County, Pennsylvania. Not long thereafter, he became an active participant in Methodist camp meetings and revivals. After his marriage, he united with the Presbyterian Church, since his wife was an active member of that fellowship. Later still, he served as Sunday School superintendent and Choir Director of Chicago's First Congregational Church. While "Lora Vale" brought him

31

fame and fortune, it was in the service of the Church that Bliss found the finest field for the full exercise of his many remarkable talents. A handsome man, blessed with a voice that ranged from low D to high A flat, he was a "natural" as a gospel song leader and sacred soloist for the prominent evangelists of his day. Having served at so many odd jobs during his youth, from farm worker to sawmill operator, to assistant cook in a lumber camp, he felt at home with everyone and made everybody feel equally at home in his presence. As he labored with various preachers and evangelists, he discovered that the edge of his creative powers was becoming sharpened, and soon he was dashing off words and music with almost effortless ease on the slightest provocation, and with a minimum of inspiration.

He heard Rev. Mr. Brundage preach one night on the experience of Paul before King Agrippa, describing the occasion when the King said to the Apostle, "Almost thou persuadest me to be a Christian, (Acts 26:28)". As he closed his sermon, the minister said, "He who is almost persuaded is almost saved; but to be almost saved is to be entirely lost." Bliss could hardly wait to pick up a piece of paper and a pencil, sit down at the piano and write the words and music of the familiar gospel song, "Almost Persuaded", which began:

1. "Almost persuaded" now to believe; "Almost persuaded"
   Christ to receive;
   Seems now some soul to say, "Go, Spirit, go Thy way,
   Some more convenient day On Thee I'll call."

On another occasion, Bliss was directing the singing for a series of services being conducted by the well-known lay preacher Dwight L. Moody. As he closed his message, Moody told the story of a Captain who was attempting to bring in his boat to the Cleveland harbor one very dark and stormy night. "The waves rolled like mountains," Moody said, "and not a star was to be seen in the clouded sky." He pictured the boat rocking on the violent waves, as the Captain peered through the darkness for the sight of a signal light by means of which to guide his vessel to safety. When he finally spotted a single light from the lighthouse, he turned to the pilot and asked, "Are you sure this is Cleveland harbor?" "Quite sure, sir," the pilot replied. "Then where are the lower lights?" the Captain continued. "Gone out, sir," the other man answered. "Can you make the harbor?" the Captain asked anxiously. "We must or perish, sir," the pilot replied. But, despite his strong heart and brave hand, in the darkness he missed the channel. With a resounding crash the boat piled up on the rocks and then settled slowly to a watery grave. As the congregation listened intently, Moody concluded with this admonition, "Brethren, the Master will take care of the great lighthouse; let us keep the lower lights burning." That was all Bliss needed to pen one of his most popular gospel hymns, "Let The Lower Lights Be Burning", which began:

1. Brightly beams our Father's mercy From His lighthouse evermore,
   But to us He gives the keeping Of the lights along the shore.
Chorus: Let the lower lights be burning, Send a gleam across
   the wave!
   Some poor fainting, struggling seaman, You may rescue,
   you may save.

In the same nautical vein Bliss wrote three stanzas and a chorus entitled "Pull for the shore" which included this admonition in the refrain:

Pull for the shore, sailor, pull for the shore!
Heed not the rolling waves, but bend to the oar.
Safe in the life-boat, sailor, cling to self no more!
Leave the poor old stranded wreck, and pull for the shore.

When Fleming H. Revell, of the Revell Publishing House, pre-pared to launch a new religious periodical in Chicago during the middle of the last century, he selected "Words Of Life" as the name for his new publication. At Revell's request, Bliss took his inspiration from John 6:67-68 (Jesus said, Will you also go away? to which Peter replied, To whom can we go? Thou hast the words of eternal life) and wrote three stanzas of one of his best songs, the first of which contained these lyrical lines:

1. Sing them over again to me, Wonderful words of life;
   Let me more of their beauty see, Wonderful words of life.
   Words of life and beauty, Teach me faith and duty,
   Beautiful words, Wonderful words, Wonderful words of life.

When England's famous woman hymn writer Frances Ridley

Havergal (1836-1879) wrote her very first hymn-poem, she thought so little of it that she crumpled up the piece of paper in her hand and threw it into the flames of the open fireplace in her room. A moment later, something seemed to say to her, "Get the paper out before it burns up." Acting upon that impulse, while not exactly understanding her obedience to such a strange whim, she reached into the flames and retrieved the crumpled bit of paper before it burned up. Gently straightening it out on her desk, she brushed off the scorched edges and placed the sheet in her handbag nearby. Later that same day, while visiting a poor woman in the community alms house, she again acted upon a sudden unexplainable impulse, took out the charred bit of paper and read her stanzas to the other woman. To her surprise they were welcomed with warm enthusiasm. Still later, they came to the attention of Philip Paul Bliss who set them to music, giving the world the gospel song, "I Gave My Life For Thee". Some hymnal editors considered Miss Havergal's lines too personal and too intimate as written in the first person, and altered them to read, more objectively,

Thy life was given for me, Thy precious blood was shed,
That I might ransomed be And quickened from the dead.
Thy life was given for me; What have I given for Thee?

But, as originally written, and wedded to Bliss' simple music, they are still sung throughout Christendom, and the personal pronouns with which the stanzas abound only make it more effective as a gospel hymn:

I gave My life for thee, My precious blood I shed,
That thou might ransomed be And quickened from the dead;
I gave, I gave My life for thee, What hast thou given for Me?

One afternoon during the summer of 1875, while walking through the hall to his own room in their residence at 664 West Monroe Street, Chicago, the words and music of "The Light Of The World Is Jesus" came to Bliss quite suddenly and were written down almost at once. In this song, he used a great deal of repetition, in order to impress upon the singers as well as the listeners the basic truth around which his lyrics were written. The key phrase is taken from John 8:12, in which Jesus said, "I am the light of the world." It shows Bliss' creative genius at its musical and poetic best.

1. The whole world was lost in the darkness of sin, The light of
      the world is Jesus;
   Like sunshine at noonday His glory shone in, The light of the
      world is Jesus.
Chorus: Come to the light, tis shining for thee; Sweetly the light
         has dawned upon me;
            Once I was blind, but now I can see The light of the
               world is Jesus.

The stories of the Old Testament heroes always intrigued Bliss
and he tried his hand at extolling the virtues of many of the great
men of Biblical history in a series of hymns and sacred songs.
From that period in his life came the hymn "Are Your Windows
Open Toward Jerusalem?" suggested by the story of Daniel who
refused to obey the edict of the King, and daily opened the windows of his room and prayed toward Jerusalem (Daniel 6:10).
From the story of the exploits of Jonathan and his armour-bearer
(I Samuel 14), he was inspired to write "Only An Armour-
bearer". The account of Daniel and his friends insisting that they
did not want to eat the rich food and drink the rare wine of the
King's table during their captivity in Babylon suggested the children's favorite "Dare To Be A Daniel" (Daniel 1:8-16). This
however was not his most popular song for children. The one
that claims that honor is "I Am So Glad That Jesus Loves Me".
In June 1870, Mr. and Mrs. Bliss were the guests of Major and
Mrs. D. W. Whittle, at their home at 43 South May Street in
Chicago. One morning Mrs. Bliss came down to breakfast and
greeted the others with the announcement that "Last evening
Mr. Bliss had a tune given to him that I think is going to live
and be one of the most used that he has written. I have been
singing it all the morning myself and cannot get it out of my
mind." At the urging of the others, she sang a stanza and chorus
of the new children's hymn. Bliss later explained that the idea for
the song was suggested by the fact that the peace and comfort
of the Christian are not founded upon his loving Christ but upon
Christ's love for him. It was in that spirit that he had written:
1. I am so glad that our Father in heaven Tells of His love in
      the Book He has given;
   Wonderful things in the Bible I see: This is the dearest that
      Jesus loves me.

35

Chorus: I am so glad that Jesus loves me, Jesus loves me, Jesus
         loves me;
         I am so glad that Jesus loves me; Jesus loves even me.

This hymn now shares with William Bradbury's "Jesus Loves Me,
This I Know" the distinction of being the favorites of Christian
children the world over. Appropriately the name of Bliss' tune
is "Gladness".

During the winter of 1869-1870, Bliss heard the great English
preacher, Henry Moorhouse, preach a series of sermons on John
3:16, "For God so loved the world that he gave his only begotten
son, that whosoever believeth on him should not perish but have
everlasting life". The sermon on the one word "Whosoever" so
impressed him that he composed the song "Whosoever Will",

1. Whosoever heareth, shout, shout the sound!
   Spread the blessed tidings all the world around;
   Tell the joyful news wherever man is found: Whosoever Will
     may come.
Chorus: Whosoever will, Whosoever will, Send the proclamation
        over vale and hill;
         Tis a loving Father calls the wanderer home; Whosoever
         will may come.

It was in 1876, the year of his untimely death, that Bliss wrote
his great Passion Hymn, "Hallelujah! What A Saviour!" and
seldom has a poet or composer done better in just eight measures
of music. It is a vigorous hymn, not only in the imagery of the
stanzas but in the dramatic intensity of the two lines of music:

1. Man of Sorrows, what a name For the Son of God Who came
   Ruined sinners to reclaim! Hallelujah! What a Saviour!

In striking contrast is his more intimate and personal poem "My
Prayer" which he also set to beautiful music:

1. More holiness give me, More striving within;
   More patience in suffering, More sorrow for sin;
   More faith in my Saviour, More sense of His care;
   More joy in His service, More purpose in prayer.

At one stage of General Sherman's march from Atlanta to the
Sea during the Civil War, in October 1864, his army was camped
near the Georgia metropolis. General Hood's forces in a carefully
prepared movement passed Sherman's right flank, gained his

rear and began the destruction of the railroad, burning block-houses and destroying garrisons along the way. Sherman immediately began the pursuit of Hood to save his supplies, principally the large supply base at Allatoona Pass, in the Allatoona range of mountains through which the strategic railroad ran. General Corse of Illinois was stationed there with a brigade of troops composed of Minnesota and Illinois regiments. Colonel Tourtelotte was second in command of this fifteen-hundred man force, protecting more than a million and a half rations stored there. General French and six-thousand men were detailed by Hood to take Corse's position and destroy the enemy's supplies. The defenders refused Corse's order to surrender and sharp fighting commenced. Gradually Corse's forces were driven into a small fort on the crest of the hill. Just when defeat faced them, an officer caught sight of a white signal flag waving from the top of Kenesaw Mountain, twenty miles away. He signaled acknowledgement and then received this message which was relayed from mountain top to mountain top to the besieged army, "Hold the fort; I'm coming. W. T. Sherman." Under murderous fire which continued for three hours, during which General Corse himself was slain and his Colonel badly wounded, they held the fort until French was finally forced to retreat. This incident led Bliss to write his gospel song, "Hold The Fort!" with its stirring Chorus that thrilled the Church of that day:

"Hold the fort for I am coming," Jesus signals still;
Wave the answer back to heaven, "By Thy grace, we will!"

The composing of his finest hymn tune was preceded by a terrible tragedy and followed by another accident equally as tragic and as terribly fatal. When the French luxury liner "S. S. Ville du Havre" left New York harbor in November 1873, she was the most famous passenger vessel afloat. Among her passengers was Mrs. H. G. Spafford of Chicago, who, with her four children, was embarking on a long-awaited trip to the British Isles and the continent of Europe. At two o'clock on the morning of November 22, 1873, when the ship was several days at sea and sailing on quiet waters, she was rammed by the British iron sailing boat "Lochearn". Within two hours the luxurious French liner settled to the bottom of the Atlantic with the loss of two-hundred and twenty-six lives, among the casualties being the four Spafford children. Nine days later, Mrs. Spafford cabled her husband from Cardiff, Wales, "Saved Alone". His immediate reply was, "I am so glad to trust the Lord when it will cost me something". As soon as he could, Mr. Spafford booked passage on another ship and was soon crossing the Atlantic Ocean to join his grief stricken wife. On the way over, in December of that same year, 1873, the Captain invited Mr. Spafford into his cabin and said, "I believe we are now passing over the place where the Ville du Havre went down." That night Mr. Spafford could not sleep. But faith soon conquered doubt and, out of his heart-break and pain, there in the mid-Atlantic, he wrote five stanzas of a hymn which he entitled "It Is Well With My Soul." His familiar first stanza was this:

1. When peace like a river attendeth my way, When sorrows like
       sea billows roll;
    Whatever my lot, Thou hast taught me to say, "It is well, it
       is well with my soul".

When the Spaffords returned to Chicago the following year, the author requested Mr. Bliss, a friend of many years, to set his words to music. On the last Friday in November 1876, Bliss introduced the new hymn, singing it as a sacred solo at a meeting attended by more than a thousand ministers.

Early in December, just a few days after having introduced his new hymn, Bliss took his wife and their two children to visit his mother in Buffalo, New York, planning to return to Chicago by New Year's Day, when a new series of evangelistic services was scheduled to begin. Leaving their children with their grandmother, Mr. and Mrs. Bliss boarded the Pacific Express, the Lake Shore and Michigan Southern Railroad's pride and joy. Her two engines were pulling eleven passenger cars, packed with nearly one-hundred and sixty people, when she pulled out of Erie, Pennsylvania in a driving snow storm that night of December 26, 1876. Bliss and his wife spent some time in the palatial drawing room car, the Yokohama, where they visited casually with friends and acquaintances, and then marvelled at the luxurious appointments of the sumptuous Wagner Palace Sleeping Cars like the Palatine, the City Of Buffalo and the Osceo, in which some of their fellow passengers had already retired for the night.

At 7:30 o'clock that fateful evening, Chief Conductor Bernhardt Henn heard a blast from "Socrates" the engine, and knew they were rapidly approaching the seventy-six foot high railroad bridge at Ashtabula, Ohio. What he did not know was that the train would never make it safely across. Greed for gold, irresponsibility, stupidity and general incompetence were soon to have their day! "Socrates" was two-thirds of the way across the bridge when the engineer saw the headlight of the booster engine "Columbia" flash skyward and then fall out of sight. As the so-called safe iron bridge, the monumental work of a wood and stone bridge builder Amasa Stone, crumbled beneath the added weight of the crowded passenger cars, fire broke out from the shattered stoves in the sleeping cars. What the fire and flood did not succeed in destroying, the scavengers from nearby shanty-towns personally took care of in the hours following the tragedy, robbing the dead and stealing from the wounded as the police stood helplessly by.

Final tabulations listed at least ninety-two known dead, and sixty-four seriously wounded. Among the dead were Mr. and Mrs. Philip Paul Bliss. One survivor reported that he had seen Mr. Bliss crawling from the wreckage of one of the burning sleeping cars only to look around for his wife, and, not seeing her, turn back into the flaming car to die at her side. His friends gathered at the scene of the accident the following day, but by that time what fire had not consumed the scavengers had stolen, and not one single item that could be positively identified as belonging either to Bliss or his wife was ever discovered. Like the four Spafford children, Mr. and Mrs. Bliss have no earthly grave.

The bridge builder, torn with remorse, tried for the next six years to forget what had happened at Astabula. When he couldn't get it out of his mind, he blew his brains out one May afternoon in 1883, following the example of his Chief Engineer, Charles Collins, who had already considered suicide the only way out! Those passengers did not die in vain, however, for railroad bridge builders from that day on were compelled to conform to certain safety standards and specifications, while the stoves that set the falling passenger cars afire were permanently banned and new heating systems invented and installed.

Philip Paul Bliss wrote his first song at twenty-six and his last at thirty-eight. The story of James McGranahan and the gospel hymn "I Will Sing Of My Redeemer" is a fitting climax as well as an appropriate poetic conclusion to the life and rich musical ministry of this remarkable, talented and dedicated man.

When Bliss' trunk, which had been mistakenly placed on another train, finally arrived in Chicago several days later, his friends opened it, and, among other things, found the words of a new poem he had but recently completed, which contained these stirring stanzas:

1. I will sing of my Redeemer, And His wondrous love to me;
   On the cruel cross He suffered, From the curse to set me free.
2. I will tell the wondrous story, How my lost estate to save,
   In His boundless love and mercy, He the ransom freely paid.
4. I will sing of my Redeemer, And His heavenly love to me;
   He from death to life hath brought me, Son of God, with Him to be.

James McGranahan (1840-1907), a Pennsylvania farm boy who had taken up evangelistic song leading as a career, then thirty-six years of age, and reaching the zenith of his powers as a singer and composer, was selected to be Bliss' successor and to work as a co-laborer with Major Whittle, Dwight L. Moody and other evangelists of the day. One of McGranahan's first assignments was to set his predecessor's last poem to music. This he did with artistry and feeling, adding, in the style of the day, a Chorus of his own, which emphasized the principal theme of Bliss' stanzas, and thus was the popular gospel hymn "I Will Sing Of My Redeemer" born, with the composer's Chorus which contained these lines:

Sing, O Sing of my Redeemer; With His blood He purchased me;
On the cross He sealed my pardon; Paid the debt and made me free.

In 1831, when Prophet Joseph Smith founded The Church Of Jesus Christ Of The Latter Day Saints, more familiarly known as The Mormon Church, his wife, Emma, was directed to select the hymns which the saints were to sing in their services of public worship, and thus began what was to become an extensive new hymnody on the part of a new religious organization, a hymnody that came to full fruition in the sacred stanzas of Eliza Doxey Snow Smith (1804-1887). Eliza, one of Mormondom's most illustrious women, was born on January 21, 1804 in Becket, Berkshire County, Massachusetts, the grand-daughter of a Revolutionary War soldier. Her family moved to Portage County, Ohio, in 1806, but it was not until April 5, 1835, her thirty-first year, that she accepted the Mormon religion and was baptized into the new fellowship.

As a governess in the home of the founder of the faith, Joseph Smith, she "advanced in knowledge and understanding of the Gospel", dedicating her life and talents to its growth and propagation. Soon she found herself writing sacred poems that explained in detail many of the deeper truths and insights of her new faith, her writings "breathing the inspiration of a new truth and catching the glorified vision of her prophet-teacher". When the Mormons were driven out of Missouri, they settled in Illinois, establishing a town they named Nauvoo, and it was while she was living and teaching school there that Eliza Snow penned the stanzas of her most famous Mormon hymn, "O My Father". While we do not know to what tune these lines were originally sung, we do know that after James McGranahan composed his music for Bliss' last hymn, his gospel music was quickly picked up and adapted to Miss Snow's stanzas, and it is in this form that "O My Father" is now found in the approved Hymnals of the Mormon Church. Embodying many of the truths of the new religion in her stanzas, the poet wrote, among others, these lines, which are today sung to McGranahan's familiar music:

1. O my father, thou that dwellest In the high and glorious place!
   When shall I regain thy presence, And again behold thy face?
   In thy holy habitation, Did my spirit once reside;
   In my first primeval childhood, Was I nutured near thy side?
2. For a wise and glorious purpose Thou hast placed me here on earth,
   And with-held the recollection Of my former friends and birth;
   Yet, oft-times a secret something Whispered "You're a stranger here";

41

And I felt that I had wandered From a more exalted sphere.
4. When I leave this frail existence, When I lay this mortal by,
Father, Mother, may I meet you In your royal courts on high?
Then at length when I've completed All you sent me forth to
do,
With your mutual approbation Let me come and dwell with
you.

This version does not have a separate, repeatable Chorus, but uses the entire music which McGranahan composed, for both the stanzas and the Chorus, to complete the singing of each stanza, omitting one measure of the original tune from each line of his original Refrain.

When a rebellious group broke off from the parent Mormon body (one faction looking to Joseph Smith and the other to his successor Brigham Young as leader) and founded The Reorganized Church Of Jesus Christ Of The Latter Day Saints, and prepared a Hymnal of its own, poet Joseph Luff (1852-1948) wrote still another set of original stanzas to be sung to McGranahan's familiar music, since it had so endeared itself to Mormon as well as to other hearts:

1. O my people, saith the Spirit, Hear the words of God today;
Be not slothful but obedient, Tis the world's momentous day!
Unto honor I have called you, Honor great as angels know;
Heed ye then a Father's counsel And by deeds your purpose
show.
4. Get ye up then to your mountain, Zion of this closing day;
For the glory of my coming Waits to break upon your way.
Forth from thence your testimony Shall to trembling nations
go,
And the world confess that with you God has residence below.

While the doctrines of the various branches of Christendom and Mormondom seem to conflict at many points, nevertheless, the music of James McGranahan serves as a common denominator that once more makes them one, and if the tune can ever become the creed, undoubtedly the Pennsylvania farm boy who became a singing and composing evangelist will have wrought a nobler work than he ever imagined possible.

6.

FREDERIC WEATHERLY

The Holy City

In his autobiography, "Piano And Gown", published in 1926, just three years prior to his death at the age of eighty-one on September 7, 1929, at Bathwick, England, the brilliant lawyer-poet Frederic Edward Weatherly wrote, "From my earliest childhood, ships, books and music were my chief delight." Little wonder then that many of the stanzas of the hundreds of popular poems which this remarkable Britisher was privileged to pen during his long life of more than four-score years dealt with sailors and the sea. Born in the little fishing village of Portishead, in Somerset, England, on the shore of the Bristol Channel on October 4, 1848, the son of a lowly country doctor, Frederic early learned the stories of the mythical as well as the actual heroes and heroines of the countryside, tales he was later to poeticize into verses that, set to music by a wide variety of composers, became some of the most famous popular songs of the century. While the talented lad took his early education in an elementary school conducted by the three daughters of a local Baptist clergyman by the name of Crisp in the community of his birth, his gift of being able to create readable and singable stanzas was enhanced, no doubt, by the fact that he devoured the great literature of his language in his home, familiarizing himself with the noble novels and famous poems of Tennyson and Scott as well as the stirring dramas of Shakespeare and the hymns of Wesley, Watts and Newman.

When Frederic was only seven, he and his mother watched a strange ship sailing up the channel near their home, and he heard then from his mother's lips the story of Lord Raglan, Commander in Chief of England's forces during the Crimean War, whose body that vessel was then bringing home for burial. About the same time, another war veteran told the impressionable boy about a young midshipman who took a boat's crew ashore one night at Sebastopol during the Crimean conflict, in an attempt to spike the guns of the Russian enemy there, a narrative Weatherly never forgot. Many years later he versified this incident, and when his composer-singer co-worker, Michael Maybrick, set those lines to lyrical music, soon all England was singing "The Midshipmite":

'Twas in '55 on a winter's night. Cheerily, my lads, Yeo ho!
We'd got the Russian guns in sight,
When up comes a little Midshipmite. Cheerily, my lads, Yeo ho!
"Who'll go ashore tonight?" says he, "And spike their guns along with me?"
"Why, bless'ee, Sir, come along!" says we. Cheerily, my lads, Yeo ho!

Some years earlier, however, before poetic success came to him, Frederic had completed his preliminary education at the hands of the three daughters of the well-known local Non-Conformist clergyman, and had entered Hereford Cathedral School in 1859. The music at the Cathedral services opened a new world of enjoyment and expression to the young student, and it was while he was at Hereford that he first began to develop his latent talent for writing poems and making verses. It was when he attended the Hereford Assizes during those same years, that he developed his life-long love for law and decided to embark upon a legal career. At the age of nineteen, in October of 1867, he entered Brasenose College, Oxford, to prepare himself for his life's work. The great University center not only opened to the young man a new world of the mind but also showed him new vistas of artistry and culture that nurtured and nourished the hungers of his heart and soul. Inspired by all that he saw, heard and experienced, he cultivated and mastered his craft to such an extent that the making of verses thereafter was not only a matter of stern discipline but also of stimulating delight. As a student he took his first "Oxford lunch" in the room of an upper classman and soon learned that that was the very same room in which Reginald Heber as a student had written his famous Newdigate prize poem "Palestine". Heber had later become an Anglican clergyman and

44

Missionary Bishop, and had penned some of the most majestic hymns in the English language, among them "Holy, Holy, Holy", "From Greenland's Icy Mountains", "The Son Of God Goes Forth To War" and many others.

It was while he was still a university student, prior to his graduation from Oxford in 1871, that Weatherly wrote his first successful "words for music", a poem about three old maids entitled "The Maids Of Lee", which a dear musical friend Joseph Roeckel had suggested and for which Joseph himself composed the music in 1868. The poet sold his copyright to the composer, who, along with the publisher, actually made a small fortune off the new song. When Roeckel later sent the poet a handsome check as a "gracious gratuity", Weatherly confessed that "he revelled in the money as much as he appreciated the musician's recognition." This merely whetted the young lawyer's creative appetite, and, before he received his degree from England's most famous university, he had studied all the poetry possible and mastered the craft that was to be his profitable avocation for many years to come. His writings reflected the advice of one of his Oxford tutors, Walter Horatio Pater, who had often said to his talended pupil, "Don't forget, it is just as necessary to be scholarly and sincere in the simplest song as in a great epic, and a simple song may be just as artistic as the greatest epic." "The Maids Of Lee" was soon followed by another Weatherly-Roeckel success, a ballad entitled "A Message O'er The Sea" but when the lawyer-poet later teamed up with another composer, who was also a well known and popular concert singer as well, Michael Maybrick, who published his music under the pseudonym of Stephen Adams, his place in the musical and cultural life of Great Britain was assured. On the heels of their popular ballad about "The Midshipmite", the two men collaborated on a sea chanty "Nancy Lee", a rollicking poem that began:

Of all the wives as e'er you know, Yeo ho! lads, ho! Yeo ho! Yeo
  ho!
There's none like Nancy Lee, I trow. Yeo ho! Yeo ho! Yeo ho!
See there she stands and waves her hand upon the quay,
And every day when I'm away she'll watch for me,

And whisper low when tempests blow, for Jack at sea. Yeo ho!
  lads, ho! Yeo ho!
The sailor's wife the sailor's star shall be. Yeo ho! We go across
  the sea;
The sailor's wife the sailor's star shall be, The sailor's wife his star
  shall be.

Composer-singer Maybrick, who sang as Michael Maybrick
and composed as Stephen Adams, was a native of Liverpool,
England. Born January 31, 1844, he had pursued his musical
studies in Leipzig, Germany and Milan, Italy, before returning
to his native England to embark upon a round of concert tours
that soon made his name a household one to all British music-
lovers. In 1884, at the age of forty, he even toured the United
States and Canada, singing in the principal cities of both coun-
tries. He died at Buxton, England at the age of sixty-nine on
August 25, 1913. The applause which greeted the two new "sea
songs" soon had musicians vying for the honor of setting Frederic
Weatherly's poems to music, while concert singers were out-witting
one another for the privilege of introducing these new ballads to
the eager public. Weatherly himself proved to be such a capable
lawyer that soon he was instructing other young men as they
prepared themselves for the same profession. In addition, he
was honored by being called to the bar of The Inner Temple in
London in 1887, quite an honor for the son of an humble country
physician.

While the versifying barrister wrote most of his original poems
in a secular vein, he did try his hand at a sacred song on only
one occasion, but the result proved so successful that Weatherly's
"hymn" continues to be sung far and wide throughout the English-speaking world. He combined ideas suggested by verses in
The Psalms, The Gospel of Matthew and The Revelation of John,
in what he hoped would prove an acceptable Christian hymn.
Instead, in Maybrick-Adam's capable creative hands, the poem
became a well-known and widely-beloved sacred song entitled
"The Holy City".

1. Last night I lay a-sleeping, There came a dream so fair;
    I stood in old Jerusalem, Beside the temple there; (Matthew
    21:15-16)

I heard the children singing And ever as they sang,
Methought the voice of angels From heaven in answer rang:
Chorus: Jerusalem, Jerusalem, Lift up your gates and sing,
(Psalm 24:6)
Hosanna in the highest, Hosanna to your king!

2. And then methought my dream was changed, The streets no
longer rang;
Hushed were the glad Hosannas The little children sang;
The sun grew dark with mystery, The morn was cold and chill,
(Luke 23:44-45)
As the shadow of a cross arose Upon a lonely hill.
Jerusalem, Jerusalem, Hark! how the angels sing,
(Matthew 21:9)
Hosanna in the highest, Hosanna to your king.

3. And once again the scene was changed, New earth there
seemed to be. (Revelation 21:1-2)
I saw the Holy City Beside the tideless sea;
The light of God was on its street, The gates were open wide;
(Revelation 21:23-25)
And all who would might enter, And no one was denied.
No need of moon or stars by night, Nor sun to shine by day;
It was the new Jerusalem That would not pass away!
Jerusalem, Jerusalem, Sing for the night is o'er,
Hosanna in the highest! Hosanna for evermore!

In this song, if in no other, Weatherly revealed that God had
given to him the gift of writing to the "hearts of the people and
to touch the ever responsive springs of humanity". This, his only
"hymn", introduced on the concert stage by the composer himself, has now become a permanent part of the repertoire of church
Choirs as well as sacred soloists and continues to grow in popularity as it enters upon its second century of usefulness.

During the twenty years Weatherly spent at Oxford, first as a
learner and then as an instructor and teacher, he turned out many
notable poetic successes which sang their way into many an English heart. He himself admitted that he "had an extraordinary
piece of good fortune in having so many songs set to music by
Maybrick (Adams), himself a vocalist, not merely because he
sang the songs himself but because being a singer he knew how

to write vocal music." When caustic critics dubbed his writings "shop ballads", and accused them of "popularity!" the lawyer merely shrugged their criticisms aside and continued to create those poems which the average Britisher loved and made his very own. In such a spirit, Weatherly-Maybrick published "They All Love Jack", with its rousing chorus:

For his heart is like the sea, Ever open, brave and free,
And the girls must lonely be Till his ship comes back;
But if love's the best of all That can a man befall,
Why, Jack's the king of all, For they all love Jack!

Strange as it may seem, Weatherly confessed that he had never heard the lovely melody known universally as "The Londonderry Air", nor had he even heard of the music, until he was a mature and successful lawyer-poet of sixty-four! Londonderry, or Derry, as the town is also known, is a port on the Foyle River in northern Ireland, about sixty-five miles northwest of the industrial city of Belfast, and is the chief town in the Irish County of the same name. It is one of the counties that make up the part of The Emerald Isle known as Ulster, and continues to be a vital part of The United Kingdom along with the other five counties of Antrim, Down, Armagh, Tyrone and Fermanagh. Just slightly larger than the state of Connecticut, and containing a little more than five-thousand square miles of territory, the county itself is a continuation of the Scottish highlands, its rolling hills resembling the foothills of the Blue Ridge Mountains in Virginia. Now Ulster's second city, and famous as a manufacturing and seaport center, Londonderry itself once boasted a wall a mile long, erected in 1609, the remains of which comprise the most complete city wall in the British Isles.

It was in this Irish county that the lovely melody, which took its name after the region of its origin, was born, many years ago. Natives believe that the original words, long since lost, must have been those of a hauntingly beautiful love song, but by whom and for whom and to whom no one will ever know. Although many poets have attempted to write words worthy of the history and beauty of that melody, few have succeeded. Katherine Tynan Kinkson (1861-1931), known familiarly as "the blackbird's poet", whose stanzas "All In The April Evening" constitute a well-known choral anthem, tried her hand at it with a poem that began:

1. Would God I were a tender apple blossom,
   That floats and falls from off the twisted bough,
   To lie and faint within your silken bosom,
   Within your silken bosom as that does now.
   Or would I were a little burnished apple,
   For you to pluck me, gliding by so cold,
   While sun and shade your robe of lawn will dapple,
   Your robe of lawn and your hair's spun gold.

These lines, however widely used, are a bit too sentimental and somewhat too impossible to merit the favor of the singing public.

By the year 1912, the British lawyer-poet had already established himself as one of Britain's outstanding authors of popular songs with such successes as "The Holy City", "Nancy Lee", "They All Love Jack" and dozens of others set to music by singer-composer Michael Maybrick (1844-1913). But it was during this same year, 1912, that Weatherley's sister-in-law in The United States came across a copy of the music known as "The Londonderry Air" and immediately thought of her verse-writing lawyer relative back in her native England. She thereupon secured a copy of the tune and sent it post-haste to her brother-in-law, with a note to the effect that she hoped he would be able to write some suitable stanzas to fit the melody which had, by that time, become "one of her favorite pieces of music". Stranger still is the equally true fact that two years before receiving a copy of "The Londonderry Air" of Ireland by the circuitous route that saw it going from Ireland to America and then back again to England, Frederic Weatherly had written down two stanzas of a new poem which he called simply "Danny Boy". The following year, 1911, he had re-written and revised his verses a bit, and then had filed them away for "future reference". As he hummed the melody of the music sent him by his sister-in-law, he noticed that it was perfect for an eight-line poem written in alternate lines of eleven and ten syllables. Immediately he remembered the verses he had originally penned in 1910 and then revised in 1911, and,

49

in a few moments, he was singing his own stanzas to a century-old melody:

1. "Oh, Danny Boy, the pipes, the pipes are calling,
   From glen to glen and down the mountainside.
   The summer's gone and all the roses falling
   It's you, it's you must go and I must bide.
   But come ye back when summer's in the meadow,
   Or when the valley's hushed and white with snow;
   It's I'll be here in sunshine or in shadow —
   Oh, Danny boy, Oh Danny boy I love you so!"

2. "But when ye come, and all the flowers are dying,
   If I am dead, as dead I well may be,
   Ye'll come and find the place where I am lying
   And kneel and say an 'Ave' there for me.
   And I shall hear though soft you tread above me,
   And all my grave will warmer, sweeter be;
   For you will kneel and tell me that you love me,
   And I shall sleep in peace until you come to me!"

This new song was immediately accepted by Weatherly's publishers and became just one more success in a long line of songs that had included such selections as "Darby And Joan" and many others. Although other poets who had tried their hands at it and failed, expressed themselves vocally and critically of "Danny Boy", the new song survived every storm of abuse and every claim of plagiarism on the part of frustrated authors and their musical counterparts, and soon was being sung by Sinn Feiners and Ulstermen alike and by the English as well as the Irish and by Americans as well as by Britishers. These lines merely confirmed a tribute paid the poet by a friend, who said, "His songs spring from a rich fancy and a tender spirit".

———

In the December 8, 1915 issue of London's popular journal "Punch", there appeared in print for the first time a beautiful poem by a Canadian physician turned soldier, John McCrae (1872-1918), entitled "In Flanders Field", in which the poet wrote "In Flanders Fields the poppies blow Between the crosses, row on row." During the summer and early fall of the following year, 1916, sixty-eight year old Frederic Weatherly, now one of his country's most famous poets and song-writers, followed the grim struggle then being waged between the German armies and the British forces in the first Battle of the Somme, in the French province of Picardy, just south of Flanders, a fierce battle that cost both sides more than a half a million men in killed, wounded and missing. Raging for nearly five months, from July through November, 1916, the fighting ceased only when winter set in and the men on both sides became too exhausted to fight any more.

The old province of Picardy in northwest France contained the cathedral town of Amiens as well as the ancient battlefields of Agincourt and Crecy, famed in military and legendary lore, and heralded in minstrel song and troubadour story. Against the black background of that exhaustive conflict, and in contrast to the poppies of Flanders to the north, Weatherly penned what he lived to confess was "commercially the most successful words" he had ever written, the stanzas and chorus of "Roses Of Picardy", in which he pictured "Colinette with the sea-blue eyes" watching by the poplars as the "wind in the boughs above hummed the first little song of love":

"Roses are shining in Picardy, In the hush of the silver dew;
Roses are flowering in Picardy, But there's never a rose like you!
And the roses will die with the summer-time, And our roads may
   be far apart,
But there's one rose that dies not in Picardy,
Tis the rose that I keep in my heart."

First written to fit a tune composed by Herbert Brewer, Weatherly's lines were given to thirty-four year old Haydn Wood by his publisher who did not care for either the words or music. Wood, an English violinist, concert artist and composer, had been born in Slaithwaite, England, March 25, 1882, and had entered the Royal College of Music when only fifteen, with an enviable reputation as a "child prodigy" on the Isle of Man, to which his family had moved when the lad was two years of age. Subsequently he had made numerous tours as a concert artist and had composed a wide variety of music for many different vocal and instrumental ensembles. Wood composed a tune that not only met the publisher's demands but also the public's fancy, as a consequence of which, all three men made "a considerable fortune".

Although several decades have passed and other world wars have been fought since "Roses Of Picardy" was copyrighted and first published in 1916, as long as men retain their romantic natures, they will continue to recite "In Flanders Field" and remember the poppies there, and sing "Roses Of Picardy" and recall the beauty of that old province before both were ravaged by invading and defending armies. But it is encouraging to remember that God has so created His world that long after the last gun has been silenced and the last veteran laid to rest, the bloodiest battlefields in the world are green with a mantle of grass or carpeted with poppies and roses, to remind man that beauty always has the last word, and that God refuses to be mocked by permitting man to make something ugly out of a world that the Creator Himself had made "and saw that it was good".

The song poems of Frederic Weatherly continue to remind us as well that human love at its highest and best is but a dim reflection of divine love, and that The Holy City will become a reality only when the Kingdoms of this world become the Kingdoms of our Lord and of His Christ, when He shall reign for ever and ever!

7.

THOMAS TIPLADY
Above The Hills Of Time

Rev. Thomas Tiplady, England's most famous contemporary hymn writer, told me that he was inspired to write original hymns of his own when he came across a penny pamphlet containing some of the lovely verses of Scotland's poet-laureate, Robert Burns. Until that providential encounter, Tiplady had been reared on a strict diet of the sacred stanzas of John and Charles Wesley, the eighteenth century divines who had founded The Methodist Church. As he grew to young manhood, Thomas had rebelled against the poetic theology of the Church of his fathers, and had turned his back upon the Wesleyan hymnic expressions of their faith, and it was not until his chance discovery of Robert Burns that he realized that he, too, had been born with that creative poetic spark that could not be denied.

Tiplady, who was born in a Yorkshire village in England on New Years Day, 1882, of devout Methodist parents, was one of ten children. He learned quite early what it meant to "dig" for an education. For several years he worked in a cotton mill for six hours every morning in order to be able to attend school for four hours in the afternoon. At the age of thirteen he took on a full time job at a local mill, working as much as fifty-six hours a week while continuing his studies and doing his schooling and studying at night. Although he first entered the Church of England, the Anglican communion, and then became a Captain in the Church Army, he soon returned to the Methodist fold. When the Wesleyan Methodist Church accepted him as a candidate for the ministry, he entered the Richmond Theological Seminary in London in 1905, at the age of twenty-three, to prepare himself for full time Christian service. His first pastoral appointments took him to the "inner city" and crowded slum areas of the cities of Portsmouth and London, where his pioneering work among the underprivileged of these British industrial cities ushered in a new day in the long and colorful history of British Methodism.

To attract the poor children and idle young people who swarmed through the narrow, overcrowded streets of his urban parishes, and who rarely, even out of adolescent curiosity, went inside of a Church building, Tiplady began to conduct what he called "lantern services", showing color slides to illustrate great Christian truths. Soon the urchins began crowding his assembly room, and the pastor caught a vision of building and operating a Church that would minister to its constituents by means of slides as well as motion pictures, utilizing a new and rapidly growing industry and art for the glory of God as well as for the entertainment of man.

After trying almost in vain for six barren years to attract people to his Church, Tiplady began what he proudly called his "Cinema Services", and soon found his crowds growing so great that he had to ask some of the people to stay away so others could attend! The success that attended his initial efforts in this new field was so striking that the minister was invited to visit The United States in 1919, and to speak and preach in many cities in many states on behalf of the Centenary Celebration of the Methodist Foreign Mission movement in America. Following a brief term as pastor of the Buxton Road Methodist Church, Huddersfield, he was appointed Superintendent of the Lambeth Mission in London. Here again he discovered that he would have to shatter precedents and break with the traditional way of doing the Lord's work if he expected to make any impact at all upon the people of his new parish. When less than fifty worshippers showed up on Sunday morning and fewer than a hundred on Sunday night, Tiplady quickly realized that the way things had been done in times past in Lambeth would not meet the demanding needs of the new present. With daring originality, and faith that would frighten a man of little courage, Tiplady had Lambeth Chapel rebuilt at a cost of nearly $50,000 and turned it into a religious motion picture house, renaming it "The Ideal", his first "Cinema Service" being held in the rebuilt structure in 1928.

In a very short while, the new building was packed to capacity with young people and children as well as curious adults, although services were conducted during the day as well as at night. Tiplady rapidly expanded his weekday program of services and activities and the people began to respond as enthusiastically to them as to the movies. Very gradually he introduced the singing of songs when he discovered that most of the people who came to his "sacred shows" did not know any hymns whatsoever. He would throw the words of familiar songs on the screen and let the people "sing in the dark" to their heart's content, as loudly and as harmoniously or discordantly as they desired. And just as quickly the pioneering pastor realized that the hymns he thought the people ought to be singing were not appropriate to meet their present needs, being couched in the language, phraseology and theology of a bygone century. Undaunted, he dared to do what Isaac Watts and Charles Wesley had dared to do in their day for their generation. He began to write his own hymns and sacred songs for his own congregation, many of them being designed to be sung to tunes with which most of his worshippers were already familiar.

The storms that raged throughout ecclesiastical circles when the British clergyman, Rev. Isaac Watts (1674-1748), began to write his own original hymns in the language of his own day and to introduce them in services of public worship, were finally resolved in Watts' favor, although many sincere and devout believers were of the opinion that God had stopped singing when David died, and for any man to attempt to write his own original hymns was a personal affront to the "Sweet Singer of Israel". Unfortunately, David had not penned his psalms in the English tongue, nor did he write his psalms in the metrical patterns in which English-speaking poets were accustomed to express themselves. But even at that, some leading clergymen insisted that it was "holier" for the Church to sing the cheapest doggerel as long as it was David-inspired than for the Church to sing the loftiest poetry of the day if it was from the inspired pen of some English contemporary! Anyway, the fire lit by Isaac Watts came to full flame in the great hymns of Charles Wesley (1707-1788) for there has never been another hymn writer as prolific or as majestic as

Methodism's poet laureate. But just as the cantankerous conservatives of one generation berated Watts, so did their sons and grandsons criticize the hymn writers of succeeding generations. As the fathers had sneered at Wesley, when he began to write his hymns, "Who do you think you are, Isaac Watts?" so had the grandfathers shouted at Watts, "Who do you think you are, King David?" If anyone had been so bold as to have asked David, "Now who do you think you are?", undoubtedly he would have had his head cut off, because, after all, David was the King, psalmist or not! But the sons of the same sires now began to sneer at Rev. Thomas Tiplady, and shout at him the same question, "Who do you think you are, Mr. Tiplady; Charles Wesley?" When he calmly replied that he knew exactly who he was and that he was Thomas Tiplady who was writing the hymns for his own age and generation just as Wesley and Watts and, yes, even David, had done for their's, that merely enraged his enemies and made them more critical and outspoken than before. But despite the fact that some of his ecclesiastical equals and superiors vigorously objected to his practise, Tiplady continued to write because his people loved his new hymns and songs, and began to sing them as lustily as they sang the familiar popular and patriotic songs of the day. The preacher poet was encouraged by their enthusiasm to continue to write more and more. In addition to being one of the founders of the Religious Film Society of London, Tiplady became one of the most active and creative members of the British Hymn Society, in spite of the fact that one bold clerical ignoramus said to him, "Your daring to write your own hymns is an insult to the spirit of Watts and Wesley and almost amounts to a sin!" Tiplady took refuge in his knowledge of the fact that this was merely church history repeating itself.

One of the tunes which his Lambeth people loved to sing was none other than the familiar Irish melody known universally as "The Londonderry Air," which took its name from Londonderry in North Ireland, where it is supposed to have originated many years ago. The melody itself is so old that the name of its composer has been forgotten, but Londonderry itself will be remembered as the place where St. Columba founded a monastery during the middle of the sixth century, a religious center which has been a Protestant stronghold since the days of the Protestant Reformation. Although "Danny Boy" and "Would God I Were A Tender Apple Blossom" and other poems had been sung to that well-loved tune, Tiplady went those poets one better and wrote a hymn to match that lovely melody. When it was submitted to the Committee preparing the 1931 edition of The Methodist Hymnal, it was immediately and unanimously accepted for inclusion in that volume, and young people and adults soon began singing its moving lines, in which Tiplady wrote:

"Above the hills of time the cross is gleaming,
 Fair as the sun when night has turned to day;
 And from it, love's pure light is richly streaming,
 To cleanse the heart and banish sin away.
 To that dear cross, the eyes of men are turning
 Today as in the ages lost to sight;
 And so for Thee, O Christ, men's hearts are yearning,
 As shipwrecked seamen yearn for morning light."

It was my privilege to visit this distinguished clergyman and hymn writer in his humble flat at 2/2 Chester Way, in the Lambeth section of London one afternoon. I made the trip from Picadilly Circus by bus #159, finding his residence just a few steps off Kensington Road. It was during our visit that he told me of the experiences that led him to devote himself to the Londoners of Lambeth, a ministry that spanned almost half a century and brought the unconventional clergyman world renown as a pioneering pastor of the world's first Christian Cinema Church. When he showed me a picture of his Cinema Chapel crowded with more than a thousand boys and girls, I said, "Dr. Tiplady, that isn't a chapel; its a Church." Then he explained that in Great Britain the words "Church" and "Cathedral" and "Abbey" always refer to the Established, Anglican or High Episcopal Church, while the Dissenting groups, or the Non-Conformist congregations like the Methodists, Baptists, Presbyterians and other religious organizations not supported by the government, always refer to their meeting places as "Chapels, Temples or Halls". Then I recalled that the home Church of World Methodism, John Wesley's Church, is called "City Road Chapel" while the pulpit made famous by Leslie Weatherhead was always known as a "Temple", and the great downtown preaching place of British Methodism was "Westminster Central Hall".

Dr. Tiplady said to me, "An examination of modern British hymnals is like taking a walk through a graveyard". I knew that he meant that all the writers were dead, for British customs insist upon a poet dying before his finest works can be included in their official hymnals. But he continued to write as the occasion demanded, and soon he had several of his new hymns printed in a leaflet entitled "Hymns Of The Present Age", which was supplanted sometime later by an eighty-page booklet, "Hymns From Lambeth", which contained the best works from the prolific poet's pen, set to tunes that had endeared the stanzas to his growing congregation. An autographed copy of that collection inscribed by the author to this writer is among my valued possessions today. That volume contains morning and evening hymns, children's and young people's hymns, prayers as well as hymns of thanksgiving, and stanzas prepared for the different seasons and festivals of the Christian year. From Tiplady's 1932 publication, "Songs of a Cinema Church", many of his finest hymns have found a permanent place in the lives of ecumenical Christendom and in the hymnals of many different denominations, among them being "Beyond The Wheeling Worlds Of Light" and "O Men Of God, Go Forth To Win". The 1948 edition of "Masterpieces Of Religious Verse" edited for Harper's by J. D. Morrison, contains seven Tiplady poems, while the Disciples of Christ and Northern Baptist hymnals in the United States each contain six of his finest poems.

Hymnologists and editors and interested friends are trying to break down the peculiar British custom so that those who have enriched the hymnody of their own day may have the privilege of seeing their works accepted by their own countrymen during their own lifetimes.

During the tragic years of the Second World War, Tiplady's building was badly damaged by German bombs. Following the cessation of hostilities, friends rallied to his support and hymn writers and hymn societies all around the world sent money to help him rebuild his church in part, since the rebuilding of homes had first priority. The Hymn Society of America raised funds for the installation of a new pipe organ in the rebuilt structure, a fitting tribute to the English hymn writer who was to have more original hymns included in modern hymnals than any other contemporary poet.

While the study of some modern hymnals is "like walking through a graveyard", as long as the Church can produce ministers and hymn writers like Thomas Tiplady, the future of her hymnody is assured, for his sacred songs exalt Christ as the full revelation of God's love, and challenge believers of every age to "make answer to His love," expecting from them this reply, in the poet's own words, "And we will love Thee with a love undying, Till we are gathered to Thy home above."

8.

ELISHA HOFFMAN

Leaning On The Everlasting Arms   I Must Tell Jesus

Late in May, 1959, a friend in Atlanta, Georgia sent me a clipping from "The Atlanta Constitution" which contained a column by Mr. Leo Aikman who was associated with that famous journal at the time, in which the writer told about the premier performance of one of Christendom's popular gospel hymns in a little out-of-the-way country Church in northeast Bartow County, Georgia. The story so intrigued me that I wrote Mr. Aikman and asked him where he got the material for that interesting article. In return he loaned me his personal copy of a little booklet entitled "Steeple Echoes" which had been published by the Kiwanis Club of White, Georgia. It was in the pages of this little publication that I learned for the first time that Pine Log Methodist Church in Bartow County, Georgia, had indeed been the scene of the first public presentation of a gospel song that had eventually sung its way around the Christian world, and it came to pass in this manner.

Rev. Anthony J. Showalter (1858-1924), a native of Cherry Grove, Pennsylvania, where he had been born on May 1, 1858, then an effective evangelist and singer of just thirty years of age, was conducting a series of special services at Pine Log Methodist Church in 1888. In addition to his preaching, Showalter also conducted singing schools, and, some months prior to accepting the engagement to preach and sing for the Georgia congregation, he had conducted a similar series of services in Hartsells, Alabama. He told the Georgia group that during his stay in Alabama he had received letters from two men who had been pupils of his in another singing school which he had conducted a few weeks earlier in a South Carolina community. Both letters arrived on the same day and both contained the same distressing news that each writer had recently lost his wife in death, both of the deceased women having been buried just a few days prior to the writing of the two letters. As the singing evangelist sat down to write each man out of his own heart some words of counsel that would console and encourage them at the same time, he immediately thought of the promise found in Deuteronomy 33:27, "The eternal God is thy refuge and underneath are the everlasting arms". Before he completed writing his two letters of love and sympathy, there flashed into his mind the thought that there was no hymn or gospel song with which he was familiar based upon that great promise of God. "A song should be written about the everlasting arms," he said to himself, "a song that would bring comfort to others in a similar sorrow, and strengthen them in the midst of a similar distress." Before he sealed and mailed his two letters to South Carolina, Showalter himself picked out the words and melody of a Chorus which contained just these two simple lines:

Leaning, leaning, Safe and secure from all alarms;
Leaning, leaning, Leaning on the everlasting arms.

But in spite of the fact that he tried to write a suitable stanza to precede his Chorus, nothing came, so he sent his unfinished manuscript to a preacher friend who was almost twenty years his senior, Rev. Elisha A. Hoffman, a fellow Pennsylvanian, with the request that he prepare some stanzas and a suitable tune that would fit in with the music and mood of his own little Chorus. In a few days, Hoffman returned the manuscript to Showalter with the new hymn all complete, and it was from that manuscript that the singing itinerant evangelist sang the new song for the first time that memorable night in 1888 at Pine Log Methodist Church in Bartow County, Georgia. As he sang the song, both the singer and the congregation sensed that Hoffman had "done his best" with the new idea, for in his stanzas the other clergyman had said:

1. What a fellowship, what a joy divine, Leaning on the everlasting arms;
   What a blessedness, what a peace is mine, Leaning on the everlasting arms.

61

2. Oh how sweet to walk in this pilgrim way, Leaning on the everlasting arms;
   Oh how bright the path grows from day to day, Leaning on the everlasting arms.
3. What have I to dread, what have I to fear, Leaning on the everlasting arms;
   I have blessed peace with my Lord so near, Leaning on the everlasting arms.

Encouraged by the success which greeted this new gospel song, Evangelist Showalter wrote and composed others, but none received the response which welcomed "Leaning On The Everlasting Arms." Later Showalter began a music publishing house in Dalton, Georgia, but inquiries to its present-day successor, the L. A. Lee Company, Incorporated, failed to uncover anyone who recalled the former days when the singing and composing evangelist made his home in that section of the country.

Pine Log Church was ripe for a revival when Rev. A. J. Showalter arrived on the scene, because two years earlier, on Sunday, August 31, 1886, to be exact, another event of unusual historic interest had literally "shaken the Church to its rafters" and brought the congregation to its knees. The story, recently revealed by Rev. Charles Hendrix and Professor Joe Mahan, with the help of information secured by Mrs. J. A. Dorrah and Mrs. R. E. Adair of the community, states that Rev. J. H. Sullivan was in the midst of another series of revival services at Pine Log Church in late August, 1886, when he felt that the people were not responding to his ministry as they should. Consequently on the evening of Sunday, August 31, 1886, the visiting preacher prayed loud and long for his indifferent hearers, crying to the Lord this strange petition, "Lord, if it takes it to move the hearts of these people, shake the grounds on which this old building stands!" Before he could say "Amen" to his own prayer, the grounds on which the Church stood were violently shaken by a sudden earthquake, the historically famous Georgia earthquake of Sunday night, August 31, 1886. Many people immediately fell upon their knees begging for divine mercy and promising to make amends for their wicked ways and undoubtedly the visiting preacher was praying as hard as his repentant hearers. In a way, the "earthquake prayer" did some lasting good, for the people did experience a revival of religion, and within two years had built a new Church to replace the building that had been burned during the Civil War. A marker erected in 1951 in front of the little sanctuary commemorates this remarkable coincidence of the last century.

As for Pine Log Church itself, it had been founded in 1833 by a group of Methodist families who had migrated into the valley after the opening of the Cherokee section of Georgia. In 1832 the State General Assembly had created Cass (now Bartow) County but it was not until the following year that new families were able to occupy the land, most of them coming from the eastern sections of the state. In 1861 the Church grounds served as a drill field for the 23rd Georgia Regiment, while the building itself had been destroyed during the final tragic year of the Civil War. Pine Log was first connected with the Cassville Circuit, but later all of the Methodist churches in Bartow County, with twelve different preaching points, were then united into one twelve-point circuit. Later, Pine Log and White Church became a two-point charge. The Church building was remodeled in 1930 and a new concrete porch added in 1940. On Easter Sunday 1958 ground was broken for a new educational building, and the congregation of one-hundred and fifty members took on new life as they faced the future.

Rev. Elisha A. Hoffman was born in Orwigsburg, Pennsylvania on May 7, 1839 and early chose to follow in his father's footsteps and prepare himself for the Christian ministry. During his years of training and maturing, he developed a latent talent for writing hymns and gospel songs and composing lilting tunes for Sunday School stanzas that were all the rage in religious educational circles at that time. He completed his theological studies at Union Seminary in New Berlin, Pennsylvania, receiving his license to preach in 1866. That same year he courted the girl who became his wife, although she had received her college degree four years prior to his ordination as a preacher. After their marriage he entered upon a ministerial career that was to span more than half a century. After three years in their first pastorate, the Hoffmans moved to Cleveland, Ohio in 1869, where the minister assumed the editorial responsibilities of an Evangelical denominational publication entitled "The Living Epistle". Both he and his wife began to contribute bits of original verse to this and other religious journals and when the first Hoffman collection, "The Evergreen", came from the press in 1873, it contained poems and songs by Mrs. Hoffman as well as by the editor-preacher himself. This initial volume was followed by others that enjoyed equal success, "Happy Songs for the Sunday School", in 1876, and its sequel "Sunday School Songs" in 1880. It was in 1876, the year the second Hoffman book was printed, that one of the pastor's earliest popular gospel songs was copyrighted, the song "Glory To His Name" which another minister, and fellow-Pennsylvanian, Rev. John H. Stockton (1813-1877), a Methodist, set to music. Stockton will be remembered as the author and composer of the beautiful gospel song, "Only Trust Him". Hoffman's poem included these lines, for which Stockton composed his music:

1. Down at the cross where my Saviour died, Down where for
      cleansing from sin I cried;

There to my heart was the blood applied, Glory to His Name. In lines reminiscent of William Cowper's hymn "There Is A Fountain Filled With Blood", the Evangelical minister concluded his hymn with this stanza,

4. Come to this fountain so rich and sweet; Cast thy poor soul
      at the Saviour's feet;

Plunge in today and be made complete, Glory to His Name. The musician, in the style of the day, repeated the theme of the song in the Chorus and soon "Glory To His Name" was being sung far and wide and included in the song books of many denominations.

That very same year, 1876, Mrs. Hoffman passed away at the age of thirty-two and was buried in a cemetery in Cleveland. During the last decade of the nineteenth century, Rev. Mr. Hoffman served as pastor of a Church in Lebanon, Pennsylvania, a town about thirty miles from his birthplace. By that time he had already established himself as a capable and successful poet and composer. When the division among the Evangelicals came in 1894, Hoffman went with the group later known as that portion of the denomination that united with the Brethren Church to form the Evangelical United Brethren (E.U.B.) Church.

It was during his Lebanon pastorate that Hoffman was moved to write both the words and the music of his beautiful sacred song on prayer that was to become, in the judgment of many, the finest he was to create during his long life that lacked but ten years of spanning an entire century. One afternoon as he was making pastoral calls on members of his congregation he visited a home where sorrow had preceded him, and found a distraught and disheartened woman wringing her hands in grief and crying out from the depths of a broken heart, "Brother Hoffman, what shall I do, what shall I do?" The sympathetic pastor, knowing that his parishioner had already had more than her share of sadness and affliction, and conscious of the fact that she needed to unburden her soul of its increasing weight of woe, quoted one or two pertinent passages of Scripture and then added, "You cannot do better than to take all your sorrows to Jesus. You must tell Jesus."

The worried face of the distracted woman suddenly changed, and a new light came into her eyes as she said, in response to his admonition, "Yes, I must tell Jesus!" After a period of prayer, during which she told her Lord all about her troubles, confessed to Him all of her doubts and misgivings, and claimed all His promises of forgiveness, restoration and inner peace, she rose from her knees a new person. On his way home that memorable afternoon, the minister kept repeating her words over and over again, "Yes, I must tell Jesus", and he thought of other people not only within the bounds of his own parish but also all over the world who would find healing for their broken hearts if only they would take the Master at His word and share with Him all of their trials and turn over to Him all of their heavy burdens. He said later, commenting on that unusual experience, "Do you wonder that I made my way directly to my home and that God gave me the inspiration to pen this hymn?" Because that is exactly what happened. Hoffman went straight home, entered his study, picked up his pen and soon had written down the stanzas he was so shortly thereafter to set to music:

1. I must tell Jesus all of my trials, I cannot bear these burdens alone;

In my distress He kindly will help me, He ever loves and cares
    for His own.

His Chorus reaffirmed the theme of the stanzas, for it included
these words:

I must tell Jesus, I must tell Jesus, I cannot bear these burdens
    alone;

I must tell Jesus, I must tell Jesus; Jesus can help me, Jesus alone.

His other stanzas, enlarging upon the same theme, contained
these lines:

2. I must tell Jesus all of my trouble, He is a kind, compassionate
    Friend;

    If I but ask Him, He will deliver, Make of my trials quickly
    an end.

3. O how the world to evil allures me, O how my heart is
    tempted to sin;

    I must tell Jesus and He will help me Over the world the
    victory to win.

Some records show that this hymn, words and music, was first
copyrighted as early as 1894 by the Hoffman Music Company,
while others state that it was not actually copyrighted until 1898,
being renewed twenty-eight years later in 1926 as property of the
Hope Publishing Company.

Although the clergyman-composer lived ninety long and fruitful years, during which he is said to have had a hand in writing
or composing nearly two-thousand sacred songs, this one alone
is worth his entire lifetime of preaching and pastoral visiting, and
its final affirmations of faith are as pertinent today as when Hoffman first wrote his words down and set them to music.

9.

PETER P. BILHORN

I Will Sing The Wondrous Story

Sweet Peace, The Gift Of God's Love

When the gospel singer and composer Peter P. Bilhorn accepted an invitation to take charge of the music for a series of services at the First Baptist Church of North Adams, Massachusetts in 1886, he had no idea that his presence there would inspire the scholarly pastor of that Church to pen the stanzas of the only sacred song he was ever privileged to write during his remarkably long and richly eventful life of ninety-seven years. Nor did the distinguished clergyman dream that the song-leader would be instrumental in drawing out of his heart and mind the five simple stanzas of a gospel song that would eventually sing its way around the Christian world.

The North Adams Church was the second pastorate that the Baptist preacher, Rev. Francis Harold Rowley, served, his first being a six year tenure in Titusville, Pennsylvania. Rowley, the son of an honored upstate New York physician and his wife, was born in Hilton on July 25, 1854. He prepared for the ministry at the University of Rochester, where he was awarded his Bachelor of Arts degree in 1875, and at the nearby Theological Seminary. Marriage to Miss Ida A. Babcock and the acceptance of the call to serve the Titusville congregation followed. Although he was the proud possessor of the coveted Phi Beta Kappa key, his sermons were never "over the intellectual heads" of his people, since he used his learning to make the truths of the Christian Gospel real to those who were committed to his pastoral care. The fact that, in his mature years, he was invited to preach from such renowned pulpits as that of Harvard's Appleton Chapel and the University of Chicago's Rockefeller Chapel attests to the quality of his preaching as well as to the preacher's ability to transmit his message to many different types of congregations.

Strange as it may seem, Rowley's hobby was animals and his interest in the work of the Society for the Prevention of Cruelty to Animals (SPCA) dated from the earliest years of his public ministry. During his first Massachusetts pastorate, Rowley numbered among his friends a fellow-Baptist divine, Rev. Samuel Francis Smith (1808-1895), the honored author of the nation's unofficial national anthem, "America", and undoubtedly that association kindled the creative spark in the younger man's breast, although he was never to scale the poetic heights that Smith attained in his noble lyrics.

When Bilhorn arrived at North Adams to fulfill his musical obligations there, Rowley was in his third year as pastor of the First Baptist Church. The meetings began auspiciously, and seemed to be blessed of God in an unusual way as larger and larger congregations waited upon the songs of Mr. Bilhorn and the sermons of the visiting evangelist as the services progressed night after night. Bilhorn was so deeply moved by the evidence of God's presence in their midst, and by the inspiration of being instrumental in the salvation of so many souls that he suggested to the host pastor that he write a new hymn that would be worthy of the spirit of the services then capturing the community.

Although Rowley had penned several essays and miscellaneous lectures as well as sermons during his nine years as a Baptist minister, he had never turned his talents to poetry, and it was with great reluctance that he consented to try his hand at it. To his surprise, the more he thought about it, the more rapidly several phrases and lines began to come to him with almost effortless ease, the content of several of the visiting preachers' sermons providing the theme for this proposed poem. The night after Bilhorn made his suggestion, Rowley sat down to put his new stanzas on paper, and almost before he was aware of it, he had completed five four-line stanzas. Somewhat hesitantly, he showed them to Bilhorn the next day, possibly hinting that the success of the revival merited a more dignified and scholarly poem. But the song-leader quickly put him at ease, stating that he would take the new verses and set them to music before the meetings ended, adding, in the style of the day, a lilting Chorus that would emphasize the theme of the new stanzas which Rowley had recently written:

1. I will sing the wondrous story Of the Christ Who died for me;
   How He left His home in glory For the cross of Calvary.
2. I was lost but Jesus found me, Found the sheep that went astray;
   Raised me up and gently led me Back into the narrow way.
3. Faint was I, and fears possessed me, Bruised was I from many a fall;
   Hope was gone and shame distressed me, But His love has pardoned all.
4. Days of darkness still may meet me; Sorrow's path I oft may tread;
   But His presence still is with me, By His guiding hand I'm led.
5. He will keep me till the river Rolls its waters at my feet;
   Then He'll bear me safely over Where the loved ones I shall meet.

Song-leader and composer Ira D. Sankey changed Rowley's original opening phrase, which was a question, "Can't you sing the wondrous story" to the affirmation, "I will sing the wondrous story". Later on, someone else changed the second line of the second stanza to read "Threw His loving arms around me, Drew me back into the way." Bilhorn added the Chorus:

Yes, I'll sing the wondrous story Of the Christ Who died for me;
Sing it with the saints in glory, Gathered by the crystal sea.

Before the week was over, the congregation was singing the new gospel song with contagious enthusiasm, not only because of its inherent qualities but also because it had so recently come from the pen of their own thirty-two year old pastor and his guest, the twenty-five year old song-leader. In later years, several of the original stanzas were further edited, altered and changed, some of the revisions being made without the poet's personal permission. Sankey copyrighted the new song in 1887, the year after its birth, and included it in the 1887 edition of his collection, "Sacred Songs and Solos". Bilhorn himself renewed the copyright in 1914. In some modern Hymnals, Bilhorn's music has been supplanted by the stately cadences of the hymn tune "Hyfrydol", composed by the Welsh musician Rowland H. Pritchard in his early teens and first published in a Welsh Hymnal in 1855.

Rowley continued to serve different Baptist congregations until his retirement in 1910 after a ten-year pastorate at Boston's First Baptist Church. Devoting himself to his hobby, he then went to work on a book "The Humane Idea", which was published in 1912. Another book, "Horses Of Homer", followed that first success several years later. Rowley served as President of the Massachusetts SPCA for the next thirty-five years, from 1910 until 1945, acting as Chairman of the Board of the Angell Memorial Animal Hospital in Boston until his death at the age of ninety-seven on February 12, 1953, and subsequent burial at Mt. Auburn Cemetery, Cambridge, Massachusetts. He had continued to serve various other institutions during his long and active life, filling the Presidency of the American Humane Education Society and the vice-presidency of the Boston's Children's Friend Society and the New England Baptist Hospital. Alert mentally and physically despite his advanced years, he was present in his Boston office every day, conducting the affairs of the Animal Hospital with zeal and dispatch.

Bilhorn, who was seven years Rowley's junior, died in Los Angeles in his seventy-fifth year, December 13, 1936. While they never collaborated on another successful gospel song, the meeting which inspired their most popular one always lingered in the memory of the Baptist clergyman as "one of the richest and most blessed experiences of my entire ministry". Those who have been similarly blessed by means of "I will Sing The Wondrous Story" will attest to the truth of that affirmation, adding, each in his own way, his personal testimony thereto.

When Jesus gave The Great Commission to His followers, He told them to be His witnesses "unto the uttermost parts of the earth" and ever since that day twenty centuries ago, hosts of consecrated men and women have gone forth to witness for their Lord. Some of the more famous have had their names inscribed upon the scrolls of Church history, while others who never made the headlines have still wrought a good work for Jesus Christ.

It was just such an humble and nameless witnesser who, like St. Andrew of old who invited his brother Simon Peter to come with him and meet the Lord, stepped into a Chicago concert hall one afternoon to listen to a talented young singer vocalize and sing several thrilling solos. Recognizing the gifts possessed by the attractive young artist and realizing how much they could be used of God if they were dedicated to Him and His service, this witnesser introduced himself to the soloist and invited him to attend one of the revival meetings then in progress in Dwight L. Moody's Chicago Church, under the leadership of Rev. Dr. Pentecost and song-leader George Coles Stebbins. While the name of the visiting preacher may not have "rung a bell" in the mind of the twenty-year old singer, Peter P. Bilhorn, the fact that there was reputed to be an outstanding composer, singer and conductor like George Stebbins present no doubt intrigued him.

Stebbins, then thirty-six years of age, was reaching the peak of his powers as a congregational song-leader as well as a talented trumpeter, singer and composer, and it was with the thought of studying his methods and learning a thing or two from him that Bilhorn finally agreed to attend one of the evangelistic services. There was something intangible about that first meeting that Bilhorn could never quite describe to his own satisfaction, but the following night he found himself in the congregation again, and, almost in spite of himself, he discovered that he was magnetized night after night by both the preaching and the singing of the Gospel. Before he knew it, he had not missed a service for twelve consecutive nights.

Whether the unknown witnesser who invited him that memorable afternoon knew what he had accomplished or not, God did, for He had already laid His hands upon Peter P. Bilhorn and set him aside for His holy service, though the selectee was himself not yet aware of the Master's choice. Life had not been too easy for Peter Bilhorn. For several years after his birth in Mendota, Illinois, in 1861, he did not see too much of his father, since the elder man had been summoned to the colors and was serving in the Union Army during the tragic years of the Civil War. Four years after the cessation of hostilities his father died and eight year old son Peter had to quit school and help his mother try to make ends meet. Although deprived of much formal education from that time on, the youngster developed an uncanny ability to understand and read human nature, a gift that stood him in good stead when he dedicated himself to full-time Christian service years later.

In 1877, when he was a growing adolescent of sixteen, his family moved to the city of Chicago, and there his innate gifts as a singer and musician began to develop. Soon he was in demand as an entertainer and soloist and was making a fairly decent living singing in restaurants, taverns, small concert halls and beer gardens, the thought of being used of God in a remarkable manner being farthest from his mind. Then the unknown witnesser heard him rehearsing, extended the warm invitation, and, under God's providence, was an instrument in Bilhorn's conversion. On the twelfth night of the evangelistic meetings, Dr. Pentecost preached a powerful sermon on the four-word text, "Christ hath redeemed us". That capped the climax in Bilhorn's spiritual pilgrimage; he knew his search was over, and willingly and gladly surrendered himself to God as he saw Him in the person of Jesus Christ. Anxious to make his commitment effective, Bilhorn soon began to develop his musical and speaking gifts by working in several of the missions that dotted Chicago at that time, finding greater joy in that practical expression of his faith than he ever dreamed a new believer could possess. The turbulence that had filled his heart seemed to vanish and in its place he discovered a wonderful peace that he knew the world could neither give nor take away. It was almost as if Jesus had rebuked his raging winds and stormy seas by saying, "Peace, be still", and brought that marvelous miracle to pass.

To perfect his musical skills Bilhorn studied for a time under George F. Root, the well-known composer of hymns, sacred and gospel songs as well as the universally esteemed composer and author of the most popular patriotic songs of the Civil War era, and before long, Bilhorn was following in his teacher's footsteps and writing his own stanzas and composing his own original tunes as well.

72

Six years after his conversion, as he was continuing to study, learn and witness, Bilhorn was inspired to write and compose his finest gospel hymn, a song which revealed the author's own personal struggle in its autobiographical stanzas, matched with a tune that could not be improved upon, had Root, Stebbins or any other contemporary composer tried his hand at it. Bilhorn had been invited to sing one afternoon at the famous Camp Meeting being held at Ocean Grove, New Jersey, and was inspired to present his own interpretation of one of his own songs, "I Will Sing The Wondrous Story". After the benediction, one of his close friends, Mrs. Ida Stoddard Demarest, said to him, "I wish you would write a song that would suit my voice as well as your solo suits your voice." When he asked her, "What shall it be?" she replied. "Oh, any sweet piece." Changing the spelling of the last word to "peace" as a suggested title which he immediately wrote down in his notebook, Bilhorn began thinking of the requested selection, composing his tune that same evening in the home of Mr. S. T. Gordon. It was not until the following winter that he was moved to write the original stanzas with which his tune is forever happily wedded, and the inspiration came to him with jarring suddenness during a train trip from Chicago to Iowa to assist Moody and Major Whittle in a series of evangelistic services in that midwestern state. When the train stopped near Wheaton, Illinois, the passengers saw the mangled body of an old lady lying in a ditch alongside the railroad tracks. Whittle then remarked to Bilhorn, "Do you know that is all Jesus Christ left on this earth? His body rose for our justification, but His blood was left to atone for our sins." The composer then replied, "Yes, Major, and that is what gives me sweet peace, to know that His blood atones for my sins." Back aboard the train he jotted down the stanzas of what was to become his finest gospel song. As copyrighted by the poet-composer in 1887, the new song contained these lines:

1. There comes to my heart one sweet strain, A glad and a joyous refrain;
   I sing it again and again, Sweet peace, the gift of God's love.
2. Through Christ on the cross peace was made, My debt by His death was all paid;

73

No other foundation is laid For peace, the gift of God' love.
3. When Jesus as Lord I had crowned, My heart with this peace
   did abound;
   In Him the rich blessing I found, Sweet peace, the gift of
   God's love.
4. In Jesus for peace I abide, And as I keep close to His side,
   There's nothing but peace doth betide, Sweet peace the gift of
   God's love.
Chorus: Peace, peace, sweet peace, Wonderful gift from above!
    Oh, wonderful, wonderful peace; Sweet peace, the gift
    of God's love.

After working for several years as a Christian worker among the
cowboys of the "wild and wooly west", Bilhorn returned to his
first love, and devoted his talents the rest of his days to the praise
and glory of God through the ministry of music. His experiences
convinced him that someone should make a small portable organ
for use with small gatherings in homes and stores, or outdoors
and even in street services. When he could not find one to meet
his requirements, he and his brother designed and built one of
their own, a small folding organ weighing less than sixteen pounds.
In succeeding years, their instruments won world acclaim, in addition to numerous blue ribbons and gold medals at expositions
and fairs. Two nephews carry on the Bilhorn Brothers Organ
Company to this very day, their instruments being found throughout the world in hospitals and military camps, in homes and
offices, in small Churches and on the streets for outdoor services.

But Peter Bilhorn's finest monument is not the organ he designed but the song he wrote out of his own spiritual experience,
a song that reminds seekers of every age that true peace is found
only in the service of God, since it is God's gift to those who love
Him and willingly, gladly and joyously surrender themselves to
Him. In that spirit Peter Bilhorn lived and in that same spirit he
died at the age of seventy-five in Los Angeles, California, on December 13, 1936.

10.

GEORGE BENNARD

The Old Rugged Cross

The college town of Albion, Michigan, on United States Highway #94 and on Michigan State Route #99 is ninety-six miles southwest of the automobile metropolis of Detroit. Of unusual interest are the presence in this small college town of two of the Michigan Historical Commission's Registered Sites, Numbers 215 and 216. State Marker #215 is located one block beyond the Albion College campus, across the street-highway on Michigan Avenue and College Court, in front of a large three-story white clapboard house in which the Delta Tau Delta fraternity brothers now reside. It contains this interesting inscription: "THE OLD RUGGED CROSS, one of the world's best loved hymns, was composed here in 1912 by Rev. George Bennard (1873-1958). The son of an Ohio coal miner, Bennard was a life long servant of God, chiefly in the Methodist ministry. He wrote the words and music of over 300 other hymns. None achieved the fame of 'The Old Rugged Cross', the moving summation of his faith.

I'll cherish the Old Rugged Cross,
Till my trophies at last I lay down;
I will cling to the Old Rugged Cross
And exchange it some day for a crown."

State Marker #216, in front of South Hall on the Albion College campus, just two blocks from the Delta Tau Delta fraternity house, bears this inscription: "It was in the spring of 1911 that two freshmen at Albion College, Byron D. Stokes and F. Dudleigh Vernor, wrote the words and music of a song they called 'The Sweetheart Of Sigma Chi'. The song made a hit with their fraternity brothers and requests for copies came in from other chapters. Within a few years the melody and lyrics of 'The

Sweetheart Of Sigma Chi' had become familiar to people around the world." So one of the noblest hymns on Divine Love and one of the most popular songs about human love were born just one year and two blocks apart!

However, in spite of the authentic claim contained in State Marker #215, two different Churches of two different denominations in two separate states of the Union at two distinctive seasons of the year set aside a special day which they both designate "Old Rugged Cross Day".

Chronologically, the first such celebration is held on the second Sunday in January of each recurring year, at the Friend's Church in Sturgeon Bay, Wisconsin. According to cherished records in the archives of that congregation, this world-famous gospel hymn was actually sung there for the first time on January 12, 1913. In this Wisconsin version, which has been authenticated by numerous personal testimonies by reputable witnesses, Rev. George Bennard, the author-composer, was one of the invited evangelists for a series of revival services in the Friend's Church of Sturgeon Bay. On his way from his home in Albion, Michigan, to the Wisconsin community, Bennard is supposed to have strummed a few chords on his guitar and picked out the first few phrases of what was to become his most famous musical composition.

During the days of the revival, Bennard completed his song and at the insistence of the local pastor, he sang it to a small group the last afternoon of the revival services. That night, Bennard and a Nazarene pastor, Rev. E. E. Mieras, used the new number as a sacred duet, being accompanied at the piano by Miss Pearl Berg. A large plaque commemorating this dramatic event in the history of American Christendom carries this inscription, "Most Popular and widely accepted Christian hymn, The Old Rugged Cross, completed by Rev. George Bennard during evangelistic meetings here, December 29, 1912 - January 12, 1913. First sung as a quartet in the Friend's Church parlors and as a duet at the last service from penciled words and notes." Then follow the four stanzas and chorus of Bennard's masterpiece. A striking cross and the memorial plaque quoted above were erected in 1947 with contributions from many interested friends and business houses, one member of the general committee being Mr.

Henry Maples, one of the four members of the quartet who had shared in the honor of singing the hymn for the first time in a service of public worship.

The Friend's Church, with a large cross standing nearby, still serves the community of Sturgeon Bay, and the second Sunday of every January sees larger and more enthusiastic congregations assembling there to commemorate an event that had far-reaching consequences of which Bennard little dreamed as he hummed his tune, picked out his words and strummed a few simple chords on his guitar during those eventful days.

Strangely enough, the folks up Sturgeon Bay way are not alone in their services of commemoration, nor is their day the only "Old Rugged Cross Day" in America's Church calendar. For more than a score of years, the members of the Methodist Church in Pokagon, Michigan, have been setting aside June 7 as their day, and have insisted that it was in their Church in their state on their day that the hymn was first sung in a service of public worship. In fact, their memorial plaque, instead of being inscribed on a bronze tablet, has been chiseled out of stone, and contains this revealing bit of information. "'The Old Rugged Cross', composed by George Bennard, was first sung in this Church by a Choir comprised by Frank Virgil, Olive Marrs, Clara Virgil, Wm. Thaldorf, Florence Jones — Organist." Their version is that while Rev. Mr. Bennard was conducting a series of revival services in their Church for their congregation in June of 1913, he was inspired to write and compose the words and music of the nation's Number One Gospel Hymn. In fact, they point to the additional fact that he sang it for the first time as he strummed his own accompaniment on his guitar in the kitchen of the Methodist parsonage there, for the pastor and his wife, Rev. and Mrs. L. O. Bostwick, the pastor being moved to comment at the close of the last chorus, "God has given you a song that will never die. It moved us as no other song ever has."

Bennard himself, a native of Youngstown, Ohio, in his own little book entitled "The Old Rugged Cross", copyrighted 1930, states that he sang it from the manuscript to his personal friends, the Bostwicks, who were "so thrilled that they asked for the privilege of paying for having the plate made and the first copies printed." The author further states that "the first public rendition" of his new composition was at a large convention being held at the Chicago Evangelistic Institute in the Illinois metropolis.

The Pokagon congregation got going on its commemorative celebration plans in 1938, beating the Wisconsin Church by nearly a decade, and they, too, formed an association, and carefully documented all the facts of the case and held their first service in June of that year.

The only intelligent and Christian way to reconcile these conflicting dates and places is to recognize the fact that undoubtedly the song was many months in preparation. Bennard must have tried it out here and there whenever and wherever he found a group of sympathetic listeners, asking them to listen to it and then sing it with him, so as to get not only their reactions to his song but also their ideas about its possible improvement. If the Sturgeon Bay Church insists that he sang it there in January, 1913, no doubt he did, and if the Pokagon people insist that he did the very same thing in their Church in June of the same year, he certainly must have. One is almost tempted to let the Wisconsin Church have the credit for hearing the first quartet arrangement and the Michigan Church the honor of hearing the first choir arrangement, although there was but one voice added to the choral aggregation between January and June! Later the author confessed that he had been undergoing quite an extended period of spiritual struggle prior to reaching the heights of spiritual certainty which resulted in this poem, which could almost be an account of his own searching pilgrimage for the witness of the spirit in his own heart, a struggle that was the counterpart of one which Methodism's founder, John Wesley, had himself undergone over a period of many years.

That being the case, the two claims to fame on the part of the Churches concerned can be understood. The poet wrote, "I was praying for a full understanding of the cross, and its plan in Christianity. I read and studied and prayed. I saw Christ and the Cross inseparably. The Christ of the cross became more than a symbol. The scene pictured a method, outlined a process and revealed the consummation of spiritual experience. It was like seeing John 3:16 leave the printed page, take form and act out the meaning of redemption. While watching this scene with the mind's eye, the theme of the song came to me, and with it, the melody." When only the words of the theme came, he waited patiently, trying in vain on several occasions to finish the song that was trying to force its way out of his heart. When some months later he "caught a new vision of the Cross and began to see its deeper meaning, the flood-gates were loosed and opened and he was able to complete the entire song, both words and music."

When publisher-composer Charles H. Gabriel saw the manuscript, he spoke prophetically when he said, "You will hear from this song." So the most important part of the whole story was that the song finally came into existence out of the heart and soul of this dedicated minister.

Some years ago, a cartoonist, who prepares a nationally syndicated comic strip about the antics of two young men he calls "Johnny Reb and Billy Yank", had two of his fictional characters discussing their recent experiences in a Civil War prison. One soldier said, "Joe, he spent his time singing 'Camptown Races' while I spent mine singing 'The Old Rugged Cross'." I immediately wrote a letter to the well-known gentleman-artist in which I pointed out that the author and composer of "The Old Rugged Cross" had been born in Youngstown, Ohio, February 4, 1873, eight years after the close of Civil War hostilities. "If the young soldier had actually sung 'The Old Rugged Cross'", I added, "he must have been a genius, because the hymn itself was not written and composed until 1912, forty-seven years after Appomattox!" The cartoonist was kind enough to reply, admit his error and apologize for his "goof". But he is not the only one who regards "The Old Rugged Cross" as one of those "old old old hymns that Grandmother used to love." Plenty of Church people today still think that if the song was not brought over by Columbus in 1492, it must have been born along with the Authorized (King James) Version of The Holy Bible in 1611!

The death of Rev. George Bennard occasioned many an article in the religious press as well as in several prominent daily newspapers. In the columns of the Sunday, October 12, 1958, issue of The New York Times, this article appeared, under the caption "George Bennard, 85, Composer of Hymns". Dated Reed City, Michigan, October 10, and deemed important enough to be released by the Associated Press, the story spoke of the death of Rev. Mr. Bennard in a Reed City Hospital the previous Friday. The article went on to relate that the author, a retired Methodist minister of the Michigan Conference of the Methodist Church, had worked in the Iowa coal mines at the age of fifteen, to help support his widowed mother and her six children. In 1895 he was drawn to the Salvation Army at Canton, Iowa, being commissioned as an Adjutant by that organization three years later, whereupon he engaged in revival services throughout the midwestern states. He resigned that post in 1910 to undertake independent evangelistic campaigns and to devote himself to writing sacred hymns and songs. At his death he was survived by his widow, Hannah, and a Son, John Paul Bennard of Redonda Beach, California. His last sacred composition was given as "The Light On The Cross", dated 1956, commemorating the erection of a huge wooden cross near his home by the Reed City Chamber of Commerce.

Phil Kerr's Gospel Music Magazine carried an article in the November-December 1958 issue, telling of Mr. Bennard's funeral services at the Church of the Open Door in Los Angeles, California on October 17, 1958, which were conducted by Louis Talbot, Phil Kerr, Ernest Mieras and Alfred H. Ackley. Strangely enough, the same issue of that journal carried the story of the death of A. H. Ackley's brother, composer B. D. Ackley, who passed away in his late eighties on September 3, 1958, and is best known for his musical setting for "Sunrise" and "Mother's Prayers Have Followed Me". Kerr wrote that the Los Angeles City Council adjourned in respect to George Bennard's memory, a tribute to the author-composer being read during the funeral exercises by Councilman Gordon Hahn, while the music was provided by tenor soloist Ray Robles, accompanied by organist Madge Killion, with Al Sanders presiding.

While Bennard has gone to his reward, the twelve-foot high wooden cross still stands near his Reed City, Michigan, home, pointing passersby to the Cross of Jesus Christ of which Bennard had so eloquently and so beautifully sung in his poetic version of St. Paul's words "God forbid that I should glory save in the cross of our Lord Jesus Christ" (Galatians 6:14). In view of the vast influence "The Old Rugged Cross" now holds over the hearts of Christian people the world over, the precise place where and the exact time when it was written and sung seem a bit trite and insignificant, since the most important fact about the whole affair was that Bennard was exalting the Christ Whom he loved and served, and was preaching a sermon in song about the Cross upon which His Lord had suffered, bled and died. That He rose again, not only on Easter Sunday but also in the heart of George Bennard is the unanimous testimony of those who continue to be inspired by the singing of his finest gospel hymn.

* * * * *

"The Old Rugged Cross", first copyrighted for twenty-eight years in 1913, and renewed for another period of twenty-eight years in 1941, will not become Public Domain (PD) until 1969. After that date it may be included without charge in any collection of hymns and song published, unless new copyright laws are passed to the contrary in the interim. Then, no doubt, the hymn will be included in many more Hymnals and Songbooks, and reach a larger audience than it ever has to date.

* * * * *

11.

CHARLES WEIGLE

No One Ever Cared For Me Like Jesus

If, as William Congreve (1670-1729) said, hell has no "fury like a woman scorned," she has no grief like that of unrequited love. Yet out of the anguish of such a tragedy, the Old Testament prophet Hosea, whose wife, Gomer, had spurned his love and wantonly embraced a life of open sin, caught a glimpse of the "constancy and unchangeableness of the love of God for wayward man, his own experience of earthly sorrow becoming a key by means of which he tried to unlock the mystery of God's divine sorrow", the story of this pilgrimage being contained in the autobiographical Biblical book that bears the author's name.

Unfortunately, Hosea was neither the first man of God nor the last to bear upon his sensitive heart such a grievous burden. Nearly two and a half millenia later in a country far removed from the arid plains of Palestine, another man who had heard the Master's call and surrendered his life and talents to the ministry of the Church of Jesus Christ, faced the same problem which had broken Hosea's heart twenty-five centuries earlier.

Yet, when he and his childhood sweetheart had become husband and wife after a courtship of several carefree years, the thought that such an experience would eventually shatter their happiness and tear their tiny family asunder was farthest from their minds. But that actually did occur to Charles Frederick Weigle and the woman he loved, not many years after he became an itinerant evangelist, and this was the costliest price he had to pay for his loyalty to his Lord.

Charles was born in LaFayette, Indiana, on November 20, 1871, when the town's famous Purdue University was an infant school just two years old. His parents, Charles and Katherine, both German immigrants, had met in a local Methodist Church, and after a brief courtship, had married, Charles (Sr.) and his brother George, by that time, being the successful proprietors of a grocery store and bakery.

Although his father had been reared in the Lutheran tradition and his mother in the Roman Catholic Church, they both united with the Methodist Church, and reared their twelve children (five sons and seven daughters) to know God and to love the Church. Although as a lad Charles the younger got into more than his share of mischief, his mother continued to pray that God would lead her son into the field of service which He had chosen for him, her fervent petitions finally being answered when the boy was converted during his twelfth year when revival services sponsored by the local Methodist congregation were held in La-Fayette.

While he experienced the spiritual ups-and-downs common to most new Christians, he continued to "grow in grace and in the knowledge of his Lord and Saviour," although he did not decide to enter the ministry until after he had spent two years as a student at the Cincinnati Conservatory of Music in training for a full-time musical career.

Practical Christian work in churches of different denominations in Cincinnati convinced him that God had need of him as a preacher and teacher as well as a singer, so he gave up a lucrative job to sing and preach for the glory of God. His only formal training in the theological field consisted of a close and meticulous study of the sermons of some of the pulpit giants of previous generations.

Once having mastered their methods, he adapted them to his own particular style of preaching, and embarked upon an evangelistic career that was to be blessed with remarkable success in many cities, towns, and villages throughout the country. When he felt that God had called him to do the work of an evangelist, he tangled with a Methodist Bishop who insisted that Weigle, as a member of the Methodist Conference, accept an appointment to a circuit of Methodist Churches in Kansas.

Choosing to go "God's way" rather than "The Bishop's way", Charlie was tempted for a moment to sever his connection with

Methodism, but resolved his conflict by merely transferring his membership to the Methodist Episcopal Church South, (the southern branch of the then-divided American Methodism, prior to unification which took place in 1939).

Later, following a pastorate of a Friends congregation in Pasadena, California, Weigle ministered to various denominational groups, finally uniting with the Baptist Church in Sebring, Florida in 1933, the town to which he had moved eighteen years earlier, in 1915.

It was quite early during his career as an evangelist that the preacher discovered that God had given him the gift of writing gospel songs, his first sacred song, "I Am Glad I Came Home," being followed through the years by many others.

It was during his long absences from home in those first years of his itinerant ministry that Charlie's wife began to resent her loneliness and chafe beneath the burden of those long enforced separations.

Although he felt a growing alienation coming between them on this account, the minister tried his best to make their home life as pleasant and as endurable as possible under the circumstances, even moving from California to Florida in a vain and futile attempt to re-establish their life together.

But all of his efforts ended in failure. When the dreaded hour finally struck with shocking suddenness, his childhood sweetheart said to her husband and the father of their precious little daughter, "I'm leaving, Charlie; I don't want to live the life you are living. I want to go the other way — to the bright lights."

This time Weigle was too heart-broken to protest, and that very night he saw them off on a train to California.

Eight months later he ran into her on a Los Angeles street, only to have her flaunt her sinful life before him. But a few years later as she lay dying, she said to her daughter, "If you know where your father is, please ask him to pray for me, and see if God can forgive such a sinner as I."

The night they left him, Charlie almost committed suicide by hurling himself into the turbulent waters of Biscayne Bay, but God sustained him as only God can, and the distraught preacher cried, "Oh, Lord, you have taken care of me thus far. I'll go on with you till life's end."

Five years after this tragedy, and after Charlie found happiness in a second and more harmonious marriage, he was sitting at the piano in his home, fingering the keys and thinking back across the years during which God had been his strength and his song, when the phrase "No one ever cared for me like Jesus" flashed into his mind. Soon he was singing it to a tune of his own making, and before long he had completed what was to be the Chorus of his finest gospel hymn:

"No one ever care for me like Jesus; There's no other friend so
   kind as He;
   No one else could take the sin and darkness from me; Oh how
      much He cared for me."

Then, for the next half hour, he perfected his three stanzas, and before he retired that night, he had finished his greatest hymn, copyrighted by the Hall-Mack Company in 1932, two of the stanzas containing these autobiographical lines;

1. "I would love to tell you what I think of Jesus,
   Since I found in Him a friend so strong and true;
   I would tell you how He changed my life completely,
   He did something that no other friend could do.

3. Every day He comes to me with new assurance,
   More and more I understand His words of love;
   But I'll never know just why He came to save me,
   Till some day I see His blessed face above."

When blindness began to threaten him in 1958, when he was eighty-six years of age, Weigle underwent successful operations for cataracts, and, upon his recovery, continued his preaching, piano playing and singing to the glory of God, activities in which he was still engaging when I received a letter from him, post-marked, Sebring, Florida, August 16, 1960, in which, among other things, he wrote, "I am resting for a short period before returning to the Church and College" (in Chattanooga, Tennessee) where he served as a counsellor to the students.

In October 1962 he acknowledged the receipt of two of my new gospel hymns by sending me a copy of his latest, entitled "O What Glory", and added, in an attached note, "God has been very good to me in my latter years and it is a joy for me to carry on until He calls me home." A Methodist minister in Sebring, Florida, called upon Mr. Weigle at my request, and wrote, "I find him a very enjoyable and lovable old man."

Although his cup of joy has been filled to over-flowing in the intervening decades, Rev. Dr. Charles F. Weigle's noblest gospel hymn was born in the dark night of his soul, yet it has been the instrument, under God, of ushering many others into the glorious light of the Son of God, and hosts of his converts, known and unknown, could sing with him the second stanza, in which the preacher-poet confessed:

2. "All my life was full of sin when Jesus found me,
    All my heart was full of misery and woe;
    Jesus placed His strong and loving arms around me,
    And He led me in the way I ought to go."

12.

ELIZA EDMUNDS HEWITT

More About Jesus   Sunshine In My Soul   Stars In My Crown

Eliza Edmunds Hewitt had three great loves in her life: her love for her Lord, her love for the children of the Churches and Sunday Schools in which she served as a teacher for many years and her love for God's great out-of-doors. To her, "the heavens declare the glory of God and the firmament showeth his handiwork". Born in Philadelphia, Pennsylvania on June 28, 1851, the daughter of Captain James S. Hewitt and his wife Zeruiah, she remained a lifelong resident of the City of Brotherly Love and seldom has any citizen exemplified more perfectly the spirit of true fraternal affection as did Miss Hewitt during her remarkable life of nearly seventy years. In her home, the Bible was opened and read daily, while the great hymns and songs of devotion were sung from memory by the entire family. From early childhood, therefore, she was steeped in this religious atmosphere and consecrated by her parents to loyal love and service for her Lord.

After receiving her early education in the public schools of her native city, Eliza continued her studies in the Girl's Normal School there, graduating as the Valedictorian of her class. She then entered upon a career as a public school teacher in the schools of Philadelphia, and while she gave herself during the week days to the development of her students' intellects, as a faithful Sunday School teacher she cultivated their hearts and souls every Sunday. A painful spinal malady brought to a sudden and almost tragic end her career as a public school teacher, and, although it curtailed many of her Church activities, it never succeeded in crushing her spirit or destroying the contagious enthusiasm with which she always accepted her religious responsibilities. During the months of her semi-invalidism and slow recuperation, Eliza discovered that God had endowed her with the rare gift of being able to write simple but beautiful and meaningful stanzas, a talent she immediately rededicated to His glory and began to cultivate faithfully. Soon she was writing poems on a wide variety of religious subjects, in addition to turning out special programs for various seasonal Church celebrations, for Christmas, Easter, Children's Day and other such occasions. In addition she began to contribute articles to numerous religious periodicals based upon many of her experiences as a Sunday School teacher and active Church worker. Later when she had recovered sufficiently to assume some light duties in the fields nearest her heart, she became Superintendent of the Sabbath School of the Northern Home for Friendless Children, then located at Brown and Twenty-third Streets in Philadelphia, an institution closely connected with the Olivet Presbyterian Church in which she then held her membership. When she moved to another section of the city many years later, she transferred her Church membership to the Calvin Presbyterian Church, serving as Superintendent of the Primary Department of that Sunday School until her death on April 24, 1920. A co-worker who was closely associated with Miss Hewitt for the many years that she worked in Calvin Church paid her this tribute, "She demanded and received great respect from the teachers and the children. There was never a service that we were not aware that she was truly a 'child of the King'." She was so devoted to her Sunday School pupils that on one occasion when she received an invitation to deliver an address somewhere else, she wrote, "I never leave my work as Superintendent of the Calvin Primary School unless sick or out of town; it would give me great pleasure to accept your kind invitation were I not engaged at that hour."

It was during one of her recurrent periods of convalesence in 1887 that the thirty-six year old teacher made a close study of the promises of God as contained in His Holy Word, an experience that soon overflowed in the stanzas of one of her most popular gospel songs. Her earnest and sincere desire to know more about the wonderful work of her Heavenly Father and of the life and ministry of His Son, inspired her to write the four stanzas of a poetic prayer she entitled "More About Jesus":

1. More about Jesus would I know, More of His grace to others
   show;
   More of His saving fulness see, More of His love Who died
   for me.
2. More about Jesus let me learn, More of His holy will discern;
   Spirit of God my teacher be, Showing the things of Christ to
   me.
3. More about Jesus; in His Word, Holding communion with
   my Lord;
   Hearing His voice in every line, Making each faithful saying
   mine.
4. More about Jesus, on His throne, Riches in glory all His own;
   More of His Kingdom's sure increase, More of His coming,
   Prince of Peace.

Of this as well as of her hundreds of subsequent sacred songs,
her biographer writes, "She wrote exactly as she lived, loving,
tender and true, full of blessed hope and faith and good cheer."
After being closely confined to her home throughout the long
and dismal winter of that very same year, 1887-1888, her doctor
finally yielded to her insistent requests and gave her permission
to go for a short walk as soon as the bright days returned. They
could not return fast enough for Eliza Hewitt. To her, this going
out was a glorious experience, appreciated only by one who has
been prevented so long from enjoying the life-giving sunshine of
God's radiant springtime. This brief but exciting adventure not
only brought new life to her body, but also illumined her soul,
and, upon returning to her room, she immediately began to
record her impressions in the lilting stanzas that belied their author's true physical condition and disability:
1. There is sunshine in my soul today, More glorious and bright
   Than glows in any earthly sky, For Jesus is my light.
2. There is sunshine in my soul today, A carol to my King;
   And Jesus, listening, can hear The songs I cannot sing.
3. There is sunshine in my soul today, For when the Lord is
   near,
   The dove of peace sings in my heart, The flowers of grace
   appear.
4. There is sunshine in my soul today, And hope and praise
   and love,

For blessings which He gives me now, For joys "laid up" above.

John R. Sweney (1837-1899) whose varied experiences as a musician saw him a band leader during the Civil War, a music teacher in the Pennsylvania Military Academy, and finally, for more than a quarter of a century, a famous revival song leader and noted composer, set both "More About Jesus" and "There Is Sunshine In My Soul" to lilting music, adding an original Chorus that echoed the theme of each song. They proved so tremendously popular that the original copyright, secured in 1887, was renewed twenty-eight years later, in 1915.

Two years later, encouraged by the response to her first two successful sacred songs, Miss Hewitt wrote still another, which was then set to another lilting tune with a Chorus by another popular composer, William J. Kirkpatrick, a song that revealed something of the poet's own secret for joyous living, "Stepping In The Light";

1. Trying to walk in the steps of the Saviour, Trying to follow our Saviour and King;
   Shaping our lives by His blessed example, Happy, how happy, the songs that we bring.

Chorus: How beautiful to walk in the steps of the Saviour,
   Stepping in the light, Stepping in the light;
   How beautiful to walk in the steps of the Saviour,
   Led in paths of light.

Miss Hewitt spent several delightful summers at Assembly Park near Syracuse, New York, having charge of a round table there. Her friendship with the prolific blind poet Fanny Crosby began at one of these summer conferences and proved to be a richly rewarding experience for both of these remarkable and talented Christian women. It was while she was staying at the Conference center one summer that she visited the Onandaigua Tribe of Indians nearby, many of whom were active and professing Christians. She was immediately recognized and then adopted as a member of the Eel Tribe, and given an Indian name, which, being translated, meant "Carry Across". The Indians said that they wanted to honor her by making her a member of their tribe because "they enjoyed singing her hymns so much". This was the woman who, at the age of forty-six, wrote several stanzas suggested by a verse in Daniel in the Old Testament and a verse from Revelation in the New Testament. In Daniel 12:3, she read, "They that be wise shall shine as the brightness of the firmament; and they that turn many to righteousness as the stars for ever and ever". In Revelation 12:1 she found these descriptive words, "And upon her head was a crown of twelve stars." Putting these two expressions together, Miss Eliza Hewitt, wrote these colorful lines:

1. I am thinking today of that beautiful land I shall reach when the sun goeth down;
     When through wonderful grace by my Saviour I stand,
     Will there be any stars in my crown?

Chorus: Will there be any stars, any stars in my crown,
              When at evening the sun goeth down?
              When I wake with the blest in the mansions of rest,
              Will there be any stars in my crown?

2. In the strength of the Lord let me labor and pray, Let me watch as a winner of souls;
     That bright stars may be mine in the glorious day
     When His praise like the sea-billow rolls.

3. Oh, what joy it will be when His face I behold, Living gems at His feet to lay down;
     It would sweeten my bliss in the city of gold
     Should there be any stars in my crown.

These were the lines that were later to inspire composer Charles H. Gabriel to use the phrase "I'll exchange my cross for a starry crown" in his gospel song "Where The Gates Swing Outward Never". Again John R. Sweney caught the mood of her lines and set them to singable music that is still winging its way to countless hearts and encouraging untold thousands of Christians to "labor and faint not". In spite of hardships that would have completely crushed a less vigorous soul, Eliza Hewitt kept continually creative, writing, in 1898, two more well-known gospel songs, "When We All Get To Heaven" and the meditative stanzas of "Give Me Thy Heart", in which she sang:

1. "Give me thy heart," says the Father above, No gift so precious to Him as our love.

Softly He whispers wherever thou art, "Gratefully trust me
    and give me thy heart."
Chorus: "Give me thy heart, give me thy heart,"
         Hear the soft whisper wherever thou art;
         From this dark world He would draw thee apart,
         Speaking so tenderly, "Give me thy heart".

Subsequent stanzas spoke of the Son and the Holy Spirit making
the same request of each listener and hearer. Her hymns, written
with simplicity and dignity, were always "in full and perfect
accord with the Holy Scripture", so steeped was she in Biblical
truth and language. They rang with the glorious promises of God,
bringing good cheer to Christians and holding out hope for the
weary, portraying the love of Jesus in such a way as to bring
comfort and joy to countless souls. One of the most beautiful
tributes that one woman could pay another woman was paid Miss
Hewitt by one of her long-time co-workers in the Church, when
she wrote me these lines, "Like many others that are so used of
the Lord, she had no physical beauty as the world notes beauty.
She was old-fashioned in her dress but she wore the robes of
righteousness." On December 14, 1911, she sent to the mother of
a young man who had but recently passed away, a four-stanza
poem entitled "Christmas In The Father's House" which began
with these words:

Christmas in the Father's House, His first Christmas there;
All the many mansions shining In the light most fair.
All the golden harp strings ringing, All the angel voices singing,
That bright anthem once again, Once they sang o'er Bethlehem's
    plain.

When the teacher-poet was a mature and mellow Christian,
loved and respected by all who knew her, a special service in her
honor was held at her Church, Calvin Presbyterian Church,
Philadelphia, among those participating being composers B. D.
Ackley and William J. Kirkpatrick, who had set to music so many
of her beautiful stanzas. In addition, other composers, such as
E. S. Lorenz, and Homer Rodeheaver prepared musical settings
for several of her sacred poems.

The Sunday, April 25, 1920 edition of The Philadelphia Public
Ledger contained her obituary in these words, "Miss Eliza Ed-

munds Hewitt, sixty-nine years old, Sunday School worker and composer of several popular hymns, died yesterday at the University Hospital. Miss Hewitt resided at 1229 North Redfield Street. She was a sister of James E. Hewitt, member of a wholesale grocery firm; Luther E. Hewitt, law librarian at the City Hall, and Downs E. Hewitt, of a wholesale dry goods firm. She was a cousin of Edgar Page Stites, a poet, of Cape May, N. J." It was Mr. Stites who wrote the stanzas of the popular gospel song "Beulah Land" (I've reached the land of corn and wine) which John Sweney also set to music. After her death, many of her closest friends regretted that no one had ever written an appropriate answer, sequel or reply to her famous song "Will There Be Any Stars In My Crown?" But maybe it was better that no one tried, for her stanzas still serve as a constant reminder to all Christian believers and workers, teachers and pupils, men and women, preachers and laymen alike, that their primary purpose in life is to bring His jewels to Him, leaving the rewards of the future to His understanding love. "I thank God for every remembrance of her", one dear woman wrote after Miss Hewitt's death on April 24, 1920, and if her poems mirror her life, the tribute was well merited and well deserved.

13.

T. O. CHISHOLM

Great Is Thy Faithfulness
Living For Jesus   The Prodigal Son

A self-taught Methodist preacher-poet and a Methodist preacher-composer who believed that God could inspire a song as well as a sermon, collaborated to give the Christian world a gospel hymn that expressed the deepest convictions of both men's heads and hearts. The poet was Thomas O. Chisholm who was born in the traditional log cabin that later generations always associated with their political and religious heroes, in Simpson County, Kentucky, on July 29, 1866. Lacking much formal schooling, he nevertheless educated himself to such a degree that by the time he was sixteen years of age he was not only living and working on the family farm but was also teaching other children in the little rural schoolhouse where he had received what education he himself possessed.

The editor of a weekly newspaper published in nearby Franklin, Kentucky, saw possibilities in young Chisholm which others had either ignored, overlooked or failed to recognize in the first place, and he offered the twenty-one year old farm boy a position as associate editor. Thomas' acceptance of this new opportunity proved providential in a number of ways, for during the next four years he not only developed a literary style that was to stand him in good stead for more than half a century, but he also came under the influence of one of America's outstanding revivalists, Dr. H. C. Morrison, who held a series of evangelistic services in Franklin during the time that Chisholm was living and working there. One result of that series of meetings was the conversion of the young associate editor and his subsequent dedication of all of his talents to the service of the King of Kings. When Dr.

Morrison learned of the new convert's literary abilities, he immediately offered him the joint position of office editor and business manager of "The Pentecostal Herald" in Louisville, a position Thomas accepted enthusiastically, welcoming the opportunity of being more closely associated with the man who had been instrumental in bringing him into the Kingdom of God.

When Chisholm's health broke a short time after moving to Louisville, he went back to the business world, serving as a travelling salesman until he was admitted to the Louisville Conference of The Methodist Church as a travelling preacher in 1903, the same year that he was married. The ups and downs of the next two decades would have broken the heart of a man of lesser spiritual strength but they only proved to the preacher-poet that the promises of God were true and dependable. The particular promise which he and his wife claimed on numerous occasions was found in Lamentations 3:22-23, "It is of the Lord's mercies that we are not consumed, because his compassions fail not. They are new every morning; great is thy faithfulness." Shortly after his conversion, Thomas began to write sacred and religious verse, developing a latent gift that the presence of the Holy Spirit now seemed to be bringing into full flower. His first successful poem, written in 1893, was entitled "O, To Be Like Thee", and contained these opening lines, later set to music by his friend, the Irish-born composer W. J. Kirkpatrick (1838-1921), whose musical settings included such favorites as "Tis So Sweet To Trust In Jesus" and "Jesus Saves":

O to be like Thee, Blessed Redeemer, This is my constant longing and prayer;
Gladly I'll forfeit all of earth's treasure, Jesus, Thy perfect likeness to wear.

Nearly thirty years and hundreds of hymn-poems later, Chisholm, a New Jersey resident at the time, sent several sets of stanzas to the Methodist pastor-musician-composer-poet, William M. Runyan, with the request that he try his hand at giving them suitable tunes. Runyan, a native of Marion, New York, where he had been born on January 21, 1870, had early evidenced an unusual interest in music, as a result of which he had been permitted to take lessons on the melodeon when he was only seven years of age. Within five years he was serving as a Church organist, and, before graduating from high school, had established himself as a music teacher, enrolling as many as forty piano and organ pupils in his classes. He moved with his family from Marion, New York to Marion, Kansas in 1884. Feeling the call to the ministry, Runyan entered the Methodist Church and, after serving twelve years in a number of pastoral appointments, was made an evangelist of the Central Kansas Methodist Conference, a position he filled with marked success for twenty years. A poet as well as a composer, Runyan wrote his first popular hymn in 1915, naming it "Let The Fire Fall". Encouraged by Dr. D. W. Towner of "Trust And Obey" fame, he continued to exercise his creative talents, little dreaming that a few years later he would succeed Towner in the Music Department of Chicago's Moody Bible Institute.

In 1924, Runyan moved to Sulphur Springs, Arkansas, where he served the Federated Church there in addition to his outside duties as a magazine editor and a compiler of song books. Although he regarded his song-writing as a "spare time hobby", he nevertheless confessed on many occasions that "song is the finest expression of the joy of the Lord that is in every born-again Christian." When he retired after thirteen years with Moody Bible Institute, he was called "one of America's greatest contemporary writers of sacred music", while the citation accompanying his honorary Doctor of Letters' degree from Wheaton College in 1948 stated that the versatile clergyman was a "minister, editor, poet, composer of Gospel music and pianist".

Runyan looked over several of Chisholm's poems, being particularly impressed with one which began with this affirmation of the author's own personal Christian faith:

" 'Great is thy faithfulness', O God my Father,
   There is no shadow of turning with Thee;
   Thou changest not, Thy compassions, they fail not;
   As Thou hast been Thou forever wilt be."

Runyan's musical setting breathed the same note of assurance and confidence which the poet had captured in his stanzas, and it was little wonder, that, within a few years after the new gospel song had been copyrighted in 1923, it became increasingly popular throughout the Christian world. Runyan composed more than three-hundred tunes and wrote dozens of sacred poems during his remarkably long and useful life, while the Hymnals he edited for Hope Publishing Company, "Worship And Praise" in 1928, "The Service Hymnal" in 1935, and "Songs Of Hope" in 1938 enjoyed widespread sales. His friendship with the Chisholms deepened during the years and he counted it all joy when their paths were privileged to cross in the service of their Lord.

Following his retirement in 1948, the Runyans moved to Galveston, Texas, where they became so widely known and well-loved that the First Methodist Church in which they labored and worshipped set aside a special day each year in their honor. Rev. T. O. Chisholm sent me a copy of Runyan's last poem, four stanzas entitled "Remembrance", adding a note to the effect that the author had sugar diabetes and his wife, whom he had married in Marion, Kansas, August 19, 1891, was then suffering from cancer when he had penned those final lines. Speaking of his wife's illness, Runyan wrote Chisholm, "She knows it, but it would do you good to see and hear her radiant testimony", and he promised to write his friend and tell him of her passing, but was unable to fulfil that promise. She died on July 22, 1957, in Galveston, Texas, and her husband accompanied her body to its final resting place in Kansas. The morning after her burial, he arose, felt dizzy, fell, fractured his hip, was hospitalized and died in a coma exactly one week after she had preceded him to glory, on July 30, 1957, survived by their two daughters and four sons. In his "swan song", Runyan had sent these words to his friend Chisholm,

"Tis sweet to be remembered when the distance
Has thrown its weary miles twixt friend and friend;
And memory lends a dear and sweet assistance
To make life's journey happy to the end."

Among important press releases in March 1960 was one that contained these lines, "Thomas Chisholm, author of 1,200 Protestant hymns and devotional verses, many of which were used by Billy Sunday and Homer Rodeheaver, and are now favorites of Billy Graham, died at Ocean Grove, New Jersey, March 1, 1960, at the age of 93." Undoubtedly the prolific preacher-poet passed

away in the assurance of faith, for he had written in the last verse of one of his finest hymns, these words:
"Great is thy faithfulness, Great is thy faithfulness,
  Morning by morning new mercies I see;
  All I have needed thy hand hath provided;
  Great is thy faithfulness, Lord, unto me."

The fact that "Living For Jesus" has become universally popular is due in no small measure to the perfect wedding of the words and music, although the tune itself preceded the stanzas by many months and was originally composed for an entirely different poem. Interestingly enough, the music was composed by a loyal Methodist who, for thirteen years, was Music Editor of the Reformed Church in America and later for twenty-eight years served as Minister of Music for a large New Jersey Baptist Church.

To the credit of composer C. Harold Lowden are more than four-thousand musical compositions but the flowering of his musical gift came as no surprise to those who knew him when he was a little lad. A native of Burlington, New Jersey, where he was born on October 12, 1883, the babe was practically raised to music. While his mother, Emma Cherry Lowden, played the organ in the living room of their home, his father, William Henry Lowden, played the trumpet and rocked the cradle in which baby Harold lay. Doubtless the infant was as much soothed by the gentle rocking as he was startled by the sharp notes of his amateur musician father's instrument. The music must have made its impression, however, for by the time Harold was five, he was taking lessons on a half-sized violin, his father early recognizing the boy's remarkable innate talent. Soon thereafter, the boy was playing in the Sunday School orchestra, the only youngster among all of the regular oldsters, but he held his own with them in a surprising way, and, by the time he was thirteen, was serving as their conductor as well!

Harold wanted to become a composer of religious music following his family's removal to Camden, New Jersey, and the thing that actually convinced him that God had chosen him for that particular profession was a check for $2.50 which he received from the Hall-Mack Publishing Company of Philadelphia for one of his original compositions. When the publisher asked for more of the same, young Lowden was more than willing, and later, when he was invited to become a full-time employee of the publisher, he turned his back upon a successful position with a large insurance company and, for five years, was connected with the Hall-Mack Company. In striking contrast, the man who was to make Lowden's finest hymn tune acceptable with his original stanzas, Rev. Thomas O. Chisholm (1866-1960) had to leave the active ministry on account of ill-health, and became a successful insurance man instead. Feeling that he could capitalize still further on his talents as a composer and publisher, Lowden became associated with another publisher, John J. Hood, for several years before being offered the newly created position as Music Editor for the Reformed Church in The United States.

In addition to assuming the musical responsibilities of this denomination in 1913, Lowden also had oversight of the Church and Sunday School publishing departments, all of whose materials were published under the name of The Heidelberg Press. It was during the thirteen years that he was connected with the work of this Church that he was inspired to compose the tune that became his most popular as well as his most successful. But when he wrote down his music early in 1917, he felt dissatisfied with the lyrics for which he had composed it, deeming his tune worthy of more serious stanzas. Then it was that he recalled his long association with the Methodist pastor who had become a good insurance salesman, Rev. T. O. Chisholm, and wrote to him with the request that he try his hand at preparing more suitable stanzas for the recently composed hymn tune. While Lowden was thirty-four at the time, Chisholm was in his fifty-first year, and had already written the stanzas for such gospel songs as "The Prodigal Son" for which George Stebbins had composed the music, copyrighted first in 1914 by song-leader Charles M. Alexander, and "O To Be Like Thee", his first hymn, written in 1893, for which William J. Kirkpatrick had composed an original musical setting, as well as hundreds of other religious and semi-sacred songs and poems. After serving at various times as an itinerant Methodist minister, an editor of a Church journal and a travelling salesman, Chisholm had finally moved with his family to Vineland, New Jersey from Winona Lake, Indiana, not too far from the city in which his collaborator, C. Harold Lowden, made his home. When Chisholm received Lowden's music, the melody seemed to be singing out for a poem of Christian consecration and personal commitment, and, before very long, the preacher-poet was writing down these lines:

1. "Living for Jesus a life that is true; Trying to please Him in all that I do;
   Yielding allegiance glad-hearted and free; This is the pathway of blessing for me."

When he completed the Chorus, which concluded with the vow, "My life I give Henceforth to live, O Christ, for Thee alone", he felt that he had complied completely with his friend's request. Lowden concurred and copyrighted the hymn that very same year, 1917, and sent it on its way around the Christian world. The poet wrote, "The outcome seemed to justify that conclusion as this song has gone pretty well over the Christian world." Earning equal fame with this gospel hymn was his later success, "Great Is Thy Faithfulness". While the latter was inspired by an Old Testament quotation from Lamentations, the former took its inspiration from a New Testament verse, Philippians 1:21, "For to me to live is Christ".

In 1925, Lowden bought out his partner and established C. Harold Lowden Inc. a new venture that proved eminently successful until the financial crash of 1929, when the savings of many years were wiped out over night. Undaunted, the popular song-writer and composer became Minister of Music of the Linden Baptist Church, serving in that capacity for nearly a third of a century, continuing to teach, compose and arrange as he had in previous, more lucrative years. Explaining that he had no specific method of composing, Lowden stated that he "simply keeps himself ready when God speaks". Mr. and Mrs. Lowden celebrated their Golden Wedding anniversary in 1956, with their four children, two sons and two daughters, making the family circle complete. While the composer lived to see one of his compositions, "Uncle Sam's Reunion", became a player-piano favorite in the pre-juke box era, it has given him greater satisfaction to

100

know that by means of "Living For Jesus" hundreds of Christians of all ages have been inspired to dedicate themselves to the cause of Christ and His Church. No doubt for many years to come, many idealistic young people will be inspired to dedicate themselves to the full time Christian service as they sing the Chorus of Chisholm-Lowden's finest sacred song:

"O Jesus, Lord and Saviour, I give myself to Thee;
For Thou in Thine atonement Didst give Thyself for me.
I ask no other Master; My heart shall be Thy throne;
My life I give henceforth to live, O Christ, for Thee alone."

Of the many poems and sacred stanzas inspired by Jesus' Parable of the Prodigal Son as recorded in the fifteenth chapter of the Gospel of Luke, only one has become an accepted Christian hymn. Maybe it was because he felt that his life had somewhat paralleled that of the Prodigal that Thomas O. Chisholm made such a success of his sacred song on the subject. Or maybe it was due to the fact that composer George C. Stebbins (1846-1945) did such a superb job with his musical setting of Chisholm's stanzas. Be that as it may, the poet in the first poem he wrote after his conversion under the stirring sermons of the stalwart evangelist Rev. Dr. H. C. Morrison, in Franklin, Kansas, wrote these lines, inspired by John 3:3, "Except a man be born again, he cannot see the kingdom of God":

"I remember, I remember, looking back across the years,
How my foolish heart was darkened and a prey to haunting fears;
Mine, a soul without a Saviour, Mine, a life on pleasure bent;
Mine, a wayward will and stubborn, Mine, a heart impenitent."

A more graphic poetic description of a modern prodigal would be difficult to find in any field of literature, sacred or secular. Further stanzas spoke of the despondency that filled the heart of the wanderer until he wondered "whether there were hope for me". Then, "utterly despairing," he discovered Christ and found in Him the light that lifted darkness, and the salvation for which his soul had hungered.

When he began to write sacred stanzas soon after his conversion, the prolific hymn writer Fanny Crosby (1820-1915) urged

Chisholm to master the art of writing religious verses, as a result of which the poet later confessed, "I have always prized the notations and suggestions made by her". While various newspapers had clamored for his verses before he turned his talents to writing religious poetry, soon composers and hymnal editors were seeking him out, and, before he knew it, his path was crossing the paths of such famous sacred composers as W. M. Runyan, C. Austin Miles, Charles H. Gabriel, Charlie Tillman, C. Harold Lowden, George C. Stebbins and others. He felt a closer friendship with Runyan than with any of the others, however, and when the composer died on July 30, 1957, Chisholm wrote to me, "His decease has left my heart with a feeling of emptiness and loneliness from which I have not yet recovered. We loved each other so, and he was such a deep and true friend."

It was when he was meditating on the Lord's famous parable that the preacher-poet saw some similarities between his own experiences and that of the youth whom Bible readers have forever called "the prodigal son", although the Master never used that word in telling the story of the young man's life. But Chisholm saw the deeper meaning implied by Jesus' words, and quickly realized that the young man did not find himself or get on the right road until he had admitted his wrong, confessed his sins to God, as well as to himself and his father, and gone backward so that he might once again go forward on the right road. Realizing that his future progress depended upon his willingness to retrace his steps to the point of his original departure, there to start the journey of life anew, Chisholm wrote his four stanzas, the first of which contained these lines:

"Out in the wilderness wild and drear, Sadly I've wandered for
    many a year;
Driven with hunger and filled with fear; I will arise and go.
Backward with sorrow my steps to trace, Seeking my heavenly
    Father's face,
Willing to take but a servant's place; I will arise and go."

When Stebbins saw these lines, he sensed their dramatic possibilities, and began his musical setting in the minor key, modulating to the major note of assurance as he came to the Chorus, "Back to my Father and home; Back to my Father and home;
I will arise and go, Back to my Father and home."

Charles M. Alexander, the song leader and soloist who accompanied Evangelist R. A. Torrey on his preaching missions throughout the English speaking world, sang this new number as a sacred solo and thus its future was assured. Copyrighted in 1914, the song entered upon a musical ministry that saw it included in many an evangelistic singer's repertoire; rarely was it sung but that some modern prodigal, seeing the error of his sinful ways, repented, sought the Father's forgiveness, and, going "back to my father and home", prepared to embark upon a new way of life.

During his long creative life, Rev. Thomas O. Chisholm wrote poems for many different publishing houses, including Rodeheaver-Hall-Mack, Lorenz, Gospel Advocate and Gospel Trumpet among others. In 1956, Rev. Everett C. DeVelde, pastor of Covenant Presbyterian Church, Vineland, New Jersey, and a close personal friend of the aging ministerial author, selected one-hundred and sixty poems from among the more than twelve-hundred Chisholm had written during a creative career that spanned six decades and had them printed in a book appropriately entitled "Great Is Thy Faithfulness". In this volume, the words and music of his finest hymns are found, including the title hymn, "Living For Jesus", "O To Be Like Thee", and the autobiographical stanzas of "The Prodigal Son". If ever he doubted the influence of his songs, Chisholm surely was convinced that God had called him to the ministry of creative writing when he learned that Edwin O. Excell (1851-1921) the singer and composer whose finest gospel tune was composed for Johnson Oatman's stanzas "Count Your Blessings, Name Them One By One", as he lay dying in Wesley Hospital, Chicago, June 10, 1921, sang one of Chisholm's sacred songs, which the poet had called "It Is Jesus", each of the four stanzas of which had concluded with the question found in Matthew 8:27, "What manner of man is this?" To have been able to minister in such a way to an outstanding contemporary must have been satisfaction sufficient to enable the writer to continue working until God translated him from the Church militant to the Church triumphant.

14.

GEORGE C. STEBBINS

Ye Must Be Born Again

Jesus I Come To Thee   Throw Out The Lifeline

The Rev. William Washburn Sleeper (1855-1927), the Congregational minister son of a Congregational minister father, Rev. William True Sleeper (1819-1904), secured his early education at an Academy in Patten, Maine, where his father served the local Congregational Church, and then entered Phillips Academy in Exeter, New Hampshire, after which he matriculated at Bowdoin College, a liberal arts college for men at Brunswick, Maine, where he remained for only one year before transferring to Amherst College in Massachusetts for the completion of his under graduate studies. He was awarded the Bachelor of Arts degree with Phi Beta Kappa honors in 1878, enrolling that same fall in the Hartford, Connecticut, Theological Seminary from which he graduated in 1881, remaining for the next year at Hartford taking post-graduate work in theology and also serving at the same time as an instructor in music.

Young Sleeper, in addition to proving his excellence in his class work, became an accomplished organist and capable choir director. Among his original compositions was a musical setting for Miss Katharine Lee Bates' stirring poem "America The Beautiful" which the Wellesley professor had penned in 1892, a tune to which the poet herself was thereafter somewhat partial despite the popularity of the hymn tune "Materna" which Samuel Ward of Newark, New Jersey, had composed originally for the hymn "O Mother Dear Jerusalem" but which eventually became inextricably wedded to Miss Bates' sterling stanzas. On June 8, 1882, Sleeper and Miss Mabel Allen of Worcester, Massachusetts, were united in marriage in the bride's home town. Two and a half months later on August 31, 1882 to be exact, the clergy-man, at the age of twenty-seven, was ordained to the ministry of the Congregational Church. Accepting an appointment of the American Board of Commissioners for Foreign Missions of his denomination, Sleeper was then ordained as a missionary and served for the next five years as a representative of his country and his Church at the American College in Samokov, Bulgaria, returning to his native land in 1887, and assuming the pastorate of a Church in Webster, Massachusetts.

It was during the memorable year of 1882 when the young Congregational clergyman was in Worcester preparing to get married and receive ordination, that his path crossed the paths of a well known New England pastor-evangelist, Rev. Dr. George F. Pentecost of Boston, and his popular song-leader, composer George Coles Stebbins (1846-1945). At one of the night services during that memorable series, Dr. Pentecost preached an inspiring sermon on "The New Birth", taking as his text the words of Jesus to Nicodemus as recorded in John 3:3, "Verily, verily I say unto you, Except a man be born again (or anew, or from above) he cannot see the kingdom of God". As the minister developed his message on the theme of the necessity and nature of the new birth, Stebbins began toying with the idea of making a new sacred song out of the text, but quickly concluded in his own mind that the clergyman's text would result in a better song if he transferred the word "I" from the middle of the first phrase to the beginning of the phrase, making it read "I verily, verily say unto you" instead of "Verily, verily, I say unto you". At the close of the service that night, he asked Rev. William Washburn Sleeper, whom he saw in attendance, if he would be willing to try his hand at penning some original stanzas on the subject of "The New Birth" as suggested by the evangelist's sermon of the evening, utilizing the re-worded text as the Chorus. Sleeper, who by that time had already written several hymns and songs, agreed, and soon thereafter handed the visiting song-leader the stanzas which Stebbins himself soon set to music:

1. A ruler once came to Jesus by night To ask Him the way to salvation and light;

The Master made answer in words true and plain, "Ye must be born again".

Chorus: Ye must be born again, Ye must be born again;
    I verily, verily say unto you, Ye must be born again.

2. Ye children of men, attend to the word So solemnly uttered by Jesus the Lord;
And let not this message to you be in vain, "Ye must be born again".

3. O ye who would enter that glorious rest, And sing with the ransomed the song of the blest;
The life everlasting if ye would obtain, "Ye must be born again".

4. A dear one in heaven thy heart yearns to see, At the beautiful gate may be watching for thee;
Then list to the note of this solemn refrain, "Ye must be born again".

While composer Stebbins in his "Reminiscences" dates this event as taking place about 1877, when the author was still a college student at Amherst, it more than likely took place in 1882 for Sleeper was then in Worcester preparing to get married, receive ordination and go overseas as a missionary. The composer, writing about this incident, said, "Before the meetings closed, a musical setting was made, and the song was sent on its mission carrying the solemn message to the hearts and consciences of men indifferent alike to their danger and to God's claims upon them". The preacher-poet, following his experiences in Bulgaria, returned to The United States and served Congregational Churches in several communities, including Stoneham, Massachusetts, 1889-1892; Second Church, Beloit, Wisconsin, 1892-1925; and Rutland, 1925-1926. Prior to his death at the age of seventy-two in 1927, the itinerant pastor had the satisfaction of knowing that his poem had become an instrument under God of ushering many new souls into the Kingdom. His hymn and Stebbins' tune were jointly copyrighted in 1890 by the composer, the Hope Publishing Company renewing the copyright in 1918.

Two children were born to the union of Rev. William Washburn Sleeper and Miss Mabel Allen, a daughter, Helen Joy, and a son Frank.

Composer George Stebbins relates further in his "Reminiscences" that in 1887, several years after the writing of "Ye Must Be Born Again", Sleeper sent him some stanzas of "rare excellence from any point of view, and one in which the author might properly have taken great satisfaction", without any note or hint as to the occasion which prompted them or the inspiration behind them. Helen Joy Sleeper, the daughter of Rev. and Mrs. William Washburn Sleeper, who graduated from Wellesley and then served as a missionary to China, became a well known music librarian in her own right. She served her Alma Mater in that capacity for a number of years prior to her sudden death from a heart attack in 1958, just two years after her retirement, and while she was pursuing further studies in England. In a letter to the Church Music Editor of the Sunday School Board of the Southern Baptist Convention in 1954, Joy stated that the stanzas to which Mr. Stebbins referred in his last entry more than likely came from the pen of her Congregational preacher grandfather, rather than her own father, although they have been variously ascribed to each or both clergymen in the intervening years. Grandfather was Rev. William True Sleeper (1819-1904) whose chief pastorate had been a lengthy one in the village of Patten, in Aroostook County, Maine. During his extended stay in that community, Sleeper had established the town's only newspaper, "The Patten Voice", and had been instrumental in getting the Bangor and Aroostook Railroad under way in order to help the local potato farmers get their crops to market.

While Joy was convinced that both of the Sleeper poems which Stebbins set to music, "Ye Must Be Born Again" and "Jesus I Come To Thee", came from the pen of her talented grandfather, her brother, Frank M. Sleeper, wrote me that his grandfather "wrote the words of a number of hymns which had passing favor but are not now in wide use", while his father, William Washburn, was really more of a musician than a poet. Frank's letter contained the added information that more than likely the original request by Mr. Stebbins had been directed to his father, Rev. William Washburn Sleeper, who actually did write "Ye Must Be Born Again". Later the father may have sent the composer an original poem from the pen of the grandfather, Rev. William

True Sleeper, "Jesus I Come To Thee", which the musician considered a work of the son who had already done so well with "Ye Must Be Born Again" and thereafter ascribed the beautiful lyrics of "Jesus I Come" to the "wrong" Sleeper! Since William Washburn was thirty-two at the time, and his father, William True, was sixty-eight, and since the lines of "Jesus I Come" seem to have come from the pen of a more mature Christian, it is likely that Frank's statement is true, that his father had sent one of grandfather's poems to Stebbins, who assumed that the name Sleeper attached thereto meant the younger man rather than the older man, both of whom were Congregational ministers. But whether from father or son, and historians should be permitted a choice since even the grandson and grand daughter cannot agree on the actual authentic author, the stanzas do reveal an insight into the depths of Christian truth rarely equalled in any other gospel hymn before or since, for in these lines, one of the Congregational clergymen named Sleeper wrote:

1. Out of my bondage, sorrow and night, Jesus I come, Jesus I come;
   Into Thy freedom, gladness and light; Jesus I come to Thee.
   Out of my sickness into Thy health; Out of my want and into Thy wealth;
   Out of my sin and into Thyself; Jesus I come to Thee.
2. Out of my shameful failure and loss, Jesus I come, Jesus I come;
   Into the glorious gain of Thy cross, Jesus I come to Thee.
   Out of earth's sorrows into Thy balm; Out of life's storms and into Thy calm;
   Out of distress to jubilant psalm, Jesus I come to Thee.
3. Out of unrest and arrogant pride, Jesus I come, Jesus I come,
   Into Thy blessed will to abide, Jesus I come to Thee.
   Out of myself to dwell in Thy love; Out of despair into raptures above;
   Upward for aye on wings like a dove, Jesus I come to Thee.
4. Out of the fear and dread of the tomb, Jesus I come, Jesus I come;
   Into the joy and light of Thy home, Jesus I come to Thee.

Out of the depths of ruin untold, Into the peace of Thy
  sheltering fold,
Ever Thy glorious face to behold, Jesus, I come to Thee.

Rev. William Washburn Sleeper, the second generation minister, who had been born in Worcester, Massachusetts on February 12, 1855, the son of Rev. William True Sleeper and his wife,
Emily Elizabeth Taylor Sleeper, passed away in his seventy-
second year at Wellesley, Massachusetts, on March 27, 1927. Had
the two generations of Congregational clergymen collaborated
with Mr. Stebbins on these two hymns alone, their contributions
to ecumenical hymnody would have been unusually significant
and worthwhile. After the passing of three quarters of a century, both of these gospel hymns are still being widely sung, and
undoubtedly "Jesus I Come" will continue for many years in
the future to inspire those who know not the Lord to come out
of the night of their sin into the glorious light of His salvation.

As for composer and song-leader Stebbins, he gave Christendom the superb gospel tunes for such perennial favorites as "Have
Thine Own Way", "In the Secret Of His Presence", "Take Time
To Be Holy", "There Is A Green Hill Far Away", "True
Hearted", "Jesus Is Tenderly Calling", "Saved By Grace",
"Saviour, Breathe An Evening Blessing" and countless others
prior to his death in 1945, just a few months prior to his one-
hundredth birthday. When I corresponded with Mr. Stebbins in
1941 on the occasion of his ninety-fifth birthday, I little dreamed
that in the summer of 1946, just a few months after his death,
it would be my personal privilege to play and sing many of these
gospel hymns at the Chickering upright piano at which he himself had composed most of them years before. But during a
northern vacation trip that summer, our family visited the home
which Mr. Stebbins' niece had made for him in Catskill, New
York, where he had spent the last years of his long and useful
life, and this rare pleasure was there afforded me.

Fanny Crosby, the prolific writer of hymns and sacred songs,
and Will Thompson, the bard of Ohio who made a fortune composing popular songs and a reputation writing sacred songs, had
one thing in common. They both knew from their personal

experiences that the Master called them "tenderly", a striking contrast to some of the prevailing misconceptions that were widely prevalent in their day. Forgetting that Jesus had called most of His earliest followers "tenderly", some of his so-called later disciples insisted that He called people to follow Him by summoning them in a disturbing, noisy, dramatic way, thundering out His demands from the heavens in such unmistakable terms that the one being called could have no doubt but that God was addressing His celestial remarks directly to him.

"Not so", said Fanny Crosby and Will Thompson, remembering that God, Who was not present in the storm and the lightning, nor in the earthquake, came to His own through "the still, small voice" or "the breath of a light whisper." The language of love is always the whispered language, for when a lover speaks to his beloved, it is always in hushed tones, "meant for her ear alone". So when God, Who is love, speaks to His followers about His love for them, will He not as well speak in soft and whispered tones, calling to His beloved "tenderly"? So it is not surprising that both the man and the woman used the same word in describing the Master's call, Fanny Crosby writing her gospel song, "Jesus Is Tenderly Calling Thee Home", and Will Thompson going her one better by writing both the words and music of his finest musical masterpiece, "Softly And Tenderly Jesus Is Calling".

Had not George Coles Stebbins appeared on the scene to set Fanny Crosby's words to music, possibly her stanzas would have quickly been forgotten, like so many of her nearly eight-thousand hymns and sacred songs that have suffered for lack of good and appropriate tunes. But Stebbins was there when his talents were needed, and, adding a lilting Chorus in the style of the day, he gave her lines the wings of song they sorely needed to make their way through the Christian world with their warm invitation to the lost to let themselves be found of Him in Whom alone there was life, and life abundant.

George Stebbins' long life of almost one-hundred years, saw him developing from a farm boy, born in Carlton, Orleans County, New York, into one of the nation's most prominent gospel song leaders and most prolific composers of tunes for other people's religious verses. Unlike Will Thompson and Philip Bliss who could dash off words and music with equal ease, Stebbins confined himself to making music for appropriate stanzas, disciplining himself tremendously as he learned to master his chosen craft and to excel in the field of his choice.

The first musical instrument George ever saw was an accordion, called, in his day, "an elbow melodeon", played by one of the music teachers who conducted a weekly singing class in an old school house near his boyhood home. It was not until he was sixteen years old that he saw his first piano, and then it was one of those square monstrosities which cluttered up many a parlor in "those good old days beyond recall", but it awakened the genius lying dormant in the young adolescent's heart and set him on the road he was to follow joyously and productively for more than three quarters of a century. At twenty-one, when most men's voices are already set once and for all, George trudged back and forth to Buffalo once each week to take voice lessons. His early training stood him in good stead, however, because it was not very long after he mastered the art of singing in addition to his mastery of the accordion and the piano, that he began a new trend in the field of sacred music by arranging some familiar songs for a male quartet. This startling innovation captured the fancy of the Church going public and soon George was in such demand as a musician, singer, choral director and composer that he hardly knew which offer to accept.

In 1869 he moved to Chicago and assumed the musical duties at the First Baptist Church, a job that terminated suddenly when Mrs. O'Leary's cow kicked over a lantern and set the city on fire, in the process of which holocaust most of the leading Church buildings in the city were burned to the ground. Undaunted, George free-lanced as a singing evangelist for a few years, conducting meetings in many Churches of many different denominations. It was during this time that he was introduced to the unusual lay preacher, Dwight Lyman Moody, who, with his song-leader, Ira D. Sankey, was one of God's instruments for bringing about a revival of Christianity in the United States. Moody saw the genius in Stebbins and soon had him signing on the dotted line, dedicating his talents from henceforth to the service of the King of Kings. That decision, instead of hemming in the young musician, just opened new doors for the exercise of his talents that he never knew existed, and soon he was cultivating and developing his gift for setting sacred poems to original music, one that was to see him composing over fifteen-hundred original tunes prior to his death just a few months before his one-hundredth birthday.

In Boston, Stebbins gained further laurels as Choral Director of Clarendon Street Baptist Church and later at famous Tremont Temple. It was while he was serving the latter congregation that he wrote the music now associated with the evening hymn, "Saviour, Breathe An Evening Blessing", one of the best he was privileged to compose during his long and active life. His work with Moody began in 1876 and terminated only with the evangelist's death at Northfield, Massachusetts in 1899. During those busy years, Stebbins rubbed shoulders with the leading Christians of the day in America, England and in other parts of the English speaking world. Always unassuming, and loath to boast about his own accomplishments, he had highest praise for those who wrote and composed and preached, as long as they were instrumental in leading others to Christ. As an editor, his influence was felt for many years as publishing houses sought him out for advice with regard to the publication of many hymnals and gospel song books.

After Sankey's death in 1908, Stebbins retired from public life, and settled down in Brooklyn. He had married Miss Elma Miller in 1868 and to their union only one child, a son, George Waring Stebbins, had been born. But both his wife and their only son preceded him in death by many years. His last months were spent in the home of a niece in Catskill, New York, where he devoted his time to answering his heavy correspondence, advising other composers about their tunes, encouraging new musicians to dedicate their talents to the service of the Kingdom as he himself had done years before and continuing to compose almost to the very last. It was during these days that I had the personal privilege of corresponding with Mr. Stebbins and I will always cherish the letters in his own handwriting in which he thanked me for remembering him on his birthday, and commented favorably on some of my own hymns that I had sent to him for appraisal.

The Watts and Wesleys and Hebers of England wrote stanzas but no Choruses. Stebbins was one of those pioneers who saw the value of a Chorus and seldom wrote a hymn tune or gospel song melody without one. While the pendulum seems to have swung to the opposite extreme today, congregations singing Choruses without any stanzas, Stebbins, Lowry, Bliss and others ushered in a new day in Church congregational singing, writing the music that captured the imagination of the religious public and filling a need in their day that no one else was providing for. That God mightily used this group of consecrated and talented men is attested by the fact that critics said of the preaching of Moody and the singing of such men as Sankey and Stebbins, "They reduced the population of hell by a million souls." While spoken somewhat sarcastically and almost in jest, they reveal the influence of these dedicated men who gave what they had to the cause of Christ and found Him using them to a marvelous degree in His service, far beyond the reach of their fondest dreams. Because Stebbins had found in the good news of the Gospel a home for his own soul, he could compose music for Fanny Crosby's sacred song, by means of which many others found themselves coming "back home to God" as He had revealed the fulness of His nature in Christ Jesus, our Lord.

At low tide, the young Baptist preacher, Rev. Edward Smith Ufford (1851-1910), could see the wrecks of several ships from his parsonage home that overlooked the waters of the Atlantic Ocean not far from Boston, Massachusetts, and every time he gazed out across the sea and saw those huge rotting hulks of what had once been famous passenger or cargo vessels, he wondered how many lives and fortunes had been lost when those ships went down. In his mind's eye, he could picture a distraught Captain assisting with the lowering of the few, fragile crowded life-boats, while fear-filled passengers and crew members alike stood helplessly by, wondering whether the next few moments would bring rescue or death.

Ufford, who had been born in Newark, New Jersey, in 1851,

prepared for the Christian ministry at Stratford Academy in Connecticut and Bates Theological Seminary in Maine, and served several pastorates in Maine and Massachusetts before entering the evangelistic field as a full time worker. While residing in Westwood, a small town a few miles from Boston, he saw the wrecked vessels out on the sand at low tide, a vision that burned itself indelibly into his mind, to bear fruit in the strangest sort of way some years later. His interest in things pertaining to the sea led him to read widely in that field, and couple his study with observation, and before long he was visiting several life-saving stations along the coast, watching the men go through their paces and drills that would serve them to good advantage in the event that a vessel came to grief on the rocks and shoals that lurked off shore. These vivid impressions came into sharper focus several months later, when Ufford visited the life-saving station at Nantasket Beach, Massachusetts, and watched the men going through their daily drills and rehearsing every move involved in a complicated rescue mission, especially when it has to be performed under most adverse circumstances.

Watching the activities at Port Allerton that afternoon, the thirty-four year old clergyman heard the leader shout an order, "Throw out the life line", whereupon several men went through the motions involved in throwing out a line to an imaginary ship in distress beyond the breakers. At the close of the exercises, the pastor was shown a life-line with its silken strands, while every detail of its use was explained to him by a member of the life-saving crew. Later on, he listened intently as other men painted colorful and dramatic word pictures of several recent rescues in which many lives had been saved by means of the life line. When he returned to his home early that evening, all of his experiences with the sea gradually centered upon the wrecks he had been observing for so many months, and the life-saving drill he had witnessed that very afternoon. When these events suddenly began to sharpen his creative talents that evening in 1885, Christians for nearly twenty years had been singing Philip Bliss' dramatic sea-song, "Pull For The Shore, Sailor, Pull For The Shore". But Ufford was more interested in "throwing out a life line" to some sailor in distress than he was in urging the sailor to get into a life-boat and "pull for the shore". Fourteen years earlier, Rev. Edward Hopper had written himself into immortality with another great hymn on the sea, penning these lines in 1871:

Jesus, Saviour, pilot me, Over life's tempestuous sea;
Unknown waves before me roll; Hiding rock and treacherous shoal;
Chart and compass come from Thee; Jesus, Saviour, pilot me.

But Ufford sat down at his desk that evening obsessed with the idea that as a minister it was his job to throw out a life line to those in danger of drowning in the seas of sin rather than calling upon the victim to "pull for the shore" or crying out to Heaven for aid from the Master Pilot of every life. With that in mind, he began to write:

1. Throw out the life line across the dark wave; There is a brother whom someone should save;
   Somebody's brother; oh, who then will dare, To throw out the life line, his peril to share?

Chorus: Throw out the life line, Throw out the life line, Someone is drifting away!
   Throw out the life line, Throw out the life line, Someone is sinking today!

2. Throw out the life line with hand quick and strong; Why do you tarry, why linger so long?
   See, he is sinking; oh, hasten today, And out with the life-boat, away, then away!

3. Soon will the season of rescue be o'er; Soon will they drift to eternity's shore;
   Haste, then, my brother, no time for delay; But throw out the life line and save them today.

As soon as he finished his stanzas, Ufford picked out a suitable melody and soon was singing the stanzas and chorus of his new song, confessing to those who made inquiry that he had dashed the whole thing off in less than fifteen minutes. Church groups began to pick it up, and sing it here and there as well, and when composer George C. Stebbins came to Lawrence, Massachusetts the following year, 1886, to lead the singing for a series of evangelistic services, he soon heard of Rev. Mr. Ufford and his new sacred song. Seeing the possibilities in the stanzas and melody,

115

Stebbins wrote to Ufford and offered to buy his new song outright. When mutually satisfactory terms were finally agreed upon, Stebbins polished up the other man's melody and harmonized it to suit his own needs and began using "Throw Out The Life Line" as an effective sacred solo throughout the New England states. Published first in sheet music form as a sacred solo, this new selection was later included as a four-part hymn in the 1890 edition of Stebbins' own collection, "Winnowed Songs".

Many years after writing his one musical claim to fame, Ufford was visiting in California. He was invited to tell the story of the writing of "Throw Out The Life Line" at a religious service one evening. He then told the tragic tale of the sinking of the ship "Elsie Smith" off Cape Cod in 1902, and showed the worshippers a piece of the very life line that had been instrumental in the rescue of several people at the time of that tragic wreck. After the benediction that night, one of those in attendance introduced himself to the aging New England clergyman as one of the sixteen survivors whose lives had been saved by the very life line, a piece of which Ufford was still holding in his hand. Prior to his death at sixty-one, Ufford travelled widely throughout the country, presenting his story and his song in a manner that left a profound impression upon all who heard, and while he was privileged later to write and compile several books and collections of songs, this one song alone remains to perpetuate his memory.

15

LELIA NAYLOR MORRIS

Nearer Still Nearer   Sweeter As The Years Go By

During the thirty-seven years that Mrs. Lelia Naylor Morris (1862-1929) wrote and composed her gospel hymns and sacred songs, she actually produced so many that a close friend once asked her how she avoided repeating her lines, phrases, stanzas and musical melodies, to which the talented author replied, "Oh, if I feel afraid, I just run over to Will — he has a good memory — and I ask him if I have ever made that tune before." Will was one of the four children born to Mr. and Mrs. Charles H. Morris after their marriage in the Methodist Church in McConnelsville, Ohio in 1881, the other three being Fanny, the eldest, who later became the wife of Rev. Frank T. Cartwright, longtime Secretary of the Methodist Board of Foreign Missions; Will's twin sister May and Fred, the baby of the family.

Lelia, the third daughter and fifth child of John T. and Olivia Naylor, was born in 1862 in the tiny village of Pennsville, in Morgan County, Ohio. Four years after her birth, when her father returned from the Civil War, the growing family moved to Malta, Ohio, a small town midway between the city of Zanesville and the Ohio River, and it was there that Lelia was to grow up, go to school, join the Church, fall in love and marry. When she was ten years of age, Lelia joined the Methodist Protestant Church in McConnelsville. Speaking of that event years later, the poet-composer explained, "I knew that I needed a Saviour. Three different years I went forward to the altar and prayed, until a man came and laid his hand on my head and said, 'Why, little girl, God is here and ready to forgive your sins.' "

Several years after moving to Malta, and shortly after the birth of the seventh Naylor baby, John died, and the responsibility of rearing the large family suddenly fell upon Olivia's shoulders. Looking back upon those lean years, Lelia confessed, "I can remember no carefree childhood days. Always there was work to be done and every penny stretched to the limit." In addition to giving her children all the educational advantages possible under her straightened circumstances, Mrs. Naylor saw to it that her family learned the principles and practices of Christian living as well, taking them regularly to the services in the Methodist Protestant Church just across the river in nearby McConnelsville. Lelia's teachers at school found her to be a bright, discerning child, a leader in classwork as well as in outside activities, a girl sparkling with ready wit and wholesome fun. A neighbor who noticed that the young girl seemed to possess unusual musical gifts permitted her to practise on the piano in her home, and by the time she was thirteen years old, Lelia was playing the little Church organ and singing in the choir.

Church work seemed to come naturally to the young musician and singer. Cultivating her musical talents, she continued to play and sing at every opportunity. Of her "conversion" she said, "When I was ten years old, I was led to give my heart to God" and the fruit of that experience attested to its reality and sincerity. As she grew older and more mature, she assisted her mother in operating a small, successful millinery shop on the McConnelsville side of the Ohio River, learning to knit, sew, crochet and darn as rapidly as she had mastered the mysteries of the keyboard of the little Church organ.

At nineteen the inevitable happened, and she fell in love with Charles H. Morris, the son of one of McConnelville's finest families. After their wedding, the bridegroom's father built a new home for them on Kennebec Avenue, a residence they were to occupy for the next forty-seven years. After her marriage, Lelia united with the local Methodist Episcopal Chucrh in which her husband already held his membership. The difference between the Methodist Protestant and Methodist Episcopal Churches was over the matter of lay representation in Church councils and governing bodies, a divisive issue that was settled harmoniously when equal representation of clergy and laity was assured at the time that the three largest Methodist bodies in the United States re-united in 1939.

Although Mrs. Morris had revealed no particular talent for writing and composing during the first three decades of her life, a visit to a summer camp meeting ground at Mountain Lake Park in Maryland during her thirtieth year opened new doors of opportunity for her talents which Lelia never knew existed before. That memorable summer saw her experiencing another spiritual awakening, as one result of which she dedicated herself even more whole-heartedly to the service of her Christ and His Church. "I have tried to honor the Holy Spirit," she said, looking back upon that hour of re-dedication. "If we honor Him, our lives will radiate joy and gladness." To her surprise, she discovered shortly thereafter that God was going to use her to write new songs and tunes for the Christians of her own day as well as those of future generations. Soon after she had "opened her heart to let the Holy Spirit come in", she was sitting at the sewing machine in her mother's shop one day, and suddenly began to sing a simple little stanza all her very own to an equally simple little tune which was also her own creation. She walked slowly over to the piano, picked out her melody and then wrote it down along with her stanzas. Her mother encouraged her in this new venture, reminding her that her songs "were of the Spirit", and several other new songs quickly followed. The choir director of her local Church, Mr. Frank Davis, urged her to show one of her best compositions to the musical director at Mountain Lake Park, Dr. H. L. Gilmour, author of the stanzas of the gospel song "The Haven Of Rest". With his assistance, and the continued encouragement of her Malta musical co-worker, Mrs. Morris prepared a song for publication under the title, "I Can't Tell It All", and thus was her first sacred song given to the Christian world. With this humble beginning, Lelia Morris began to write and compose more hymns and sacred songs, until more than fifteen-hundred original compositions had flowed from her fluent pen.

It was in 1898 that Mrs. Morris was inspired to pen her noblest lyrics and compose her finest hymn tune, named, appropriately "Morris" in her honor. This hymn, which ranks with Mrs. Elizabeth Prentiss' "More Love To Thee, O Christ" and Ray Palmer's "My Faith Looks Up To Thee" in its devotional spirit, was entitled "Nearer Still Nearer", the first three stanzas containing these beautiful lines:

1. Nearer, still nearer, close to Thy heart, Draw me, my Saviour, so precious Thou art;
   Fold me, O fold me close to Thy breast; Shelter me safe in that 'Haven of Rest'.
2. Nearer, still nearer, nothing I bring, Naught as an offering to Jesus my King;
   Only my sinful, now contrite heart, Grant me the cleansing Thy blood doth impart.
3. Nearer, still nearer, Lord to be Thine; Sin with its follies I gladly resign;
   All of its pleasures, pomp and its pride; Give me but Jesus, my Lord crucified.

Her tune is as majestic as Spencer Lane's tune "Penitence" to which "In The Hour Of Trial" is sung, and as worshipful as Frederick Atkinson's tune "Morecambe", which is now wedded to Rev. George Croly's poem "Spirit Of God Descend Upon My Heart" and merits a far wider use than it has been afforded in recent hymnals. While Mrs. Morris never studied harmony and composition, she wrote down her tunes just as she composed them and felt that they ought to be played, her publishers rarely altering a note after receiving her manuscripts.

The late George Sanville tells the story that, during that same year, in the summer of 1898, when Mrs. Morris was then in her thirty-sixth year, she was visiting Mountain Lake Park and attending a Sunday morning service at which her friend Dr. H. L. Gilmour was directing the singing and a visiting minister, Rev. L. H. Baker, was to deliver the sermon. At the close of the stirring message on "Repentance", the preacher gave the usual invitation to those who felt moved of the Spirit to come forward and kneel at the altar, thereby signifying their desire to yield themselves to Jesus Christ as Saviour and Lord. Mr. Sanville states that a woman of obvious culture and refinement accepted the clergyman's invitation, but, as she knelt there seeking the Lord, Mrs. Morris sensed that she was undergoing a severe spiritual struggle within her own heart. Quietly rising from her seat, she joined the penitent at the altar. Putting her arm about the other kneeling woman, she said softly, "Just now your doubting give o'er". Dr. Gilmour heard the words, leaned over and added, "Just now reject Him no more." Then evangelist Baker, who had been listening to the entire conversation, stepped forward and said, "Just now throw open the door", to which Mrs. Morris added simply, "Let Jesus come into your heart". As spontaneously as that the Chorus of one of Mrs. Morris' most effective gospel songs was born. Before that particular series of services ended, she had written the four stanzas of "Let Jesus Come Into Your Heart", and composed a tune so fitting that those who sang the new song were convinced that the words and music had been created simultaneously. Her song began with this invitation,

1. "If you are tired of the load of your sin, Let Jesus come into your heart;
   If you desire a new life to begin, Let Jesus come into your heart.

Chorus: Just now your doubting give o'er; Just now reject Him no more;
        Just now throw open the door; Let Jesus come into your heart."

The two key words in the spiritual pilgrimage of Britain's famous woman hymn writer Charlotte Elliott, around which she wrote her great autobiographical hymn of invitation, were *"just as"*, for every stanza of her finest hymn began with those same two words, "Just As I Am Without One Plea". But for Mrs. Morris on the other side of the Atlantic, they were *"just now"*. While Miss Elliott was concerned with the *person* making the surrender to the Master, Mrs. Morris was interested in the *time* when that act of devotion and dedication took place.

It was in 1905 that she penned the martial strains and militant phrases of her gospel hymn "The Fight Is On, O Christian Soldier" and soon Sunday School children the country over were patting their feet as they sang enthusiastically her Chorus,

"The fight is on, O Christian soldier, And face to face in stern array,
   With armor gleaming, and colors streaming, The right and wrong engage today!
   The fight is on, but be not weary; Be strong and in His might hold fast;

If God be for us, His banner o'er us, We'll sing the victor's song
at last!"
Seven years later she wrote another song in such a different mood
that some people found it hard to believe that both songs came
from the pen of the same woman. For in that year she wrote her
sentimental favorite "Sweeter As The Years Go By", with its
familiar refrain;
"Sweeter as the years go by, Sweeter as the years go by;
  Richer, fuller, deeper, Jesus' love is sweeter, Sweeter as the years
  go by."
When her songs were being sung far and wide throughout the
Christian world, Mrs. Morris confessed, "Every writer is one of
two things, a factory or a channel. I am just a channel — I just
open my mind and let the story flow through me from somewhere
— not a factory, producing every word out of my own being."
In that spirit, this quiet, unassuming but deeply dedicated wife
and mother let herself be a channel for God's grace through the
ministry of sacred song. When her eyesight failed in 1913, she
did not give up her hymn writing, but worked as faithfully as before, despite severe handicaps, doing the things she felt God
wanted her to continue to do. Even total blindness did not pre-
vent her from writing and composing, and almost to the very end
of her life she continued singing the praises of God. It was three
years after "total darkness" had descended upon her that Mrs.
Morris wrote, in her hymn "My Choice", these revealing lines,
"Walking by faith where my eyes cannot see, I will follow Jesus;
  Holding the hand that was wounded for me, I will follow Jesus."
The janitor of her Church paid her a notable tribute when he
said, "She always seemed to be the most perfect Christian I ever
knew. In the Church she was active in almost everything."
In the fall of 1928 she moved from Ohio to make her home
with one of her married daughters in Auburn, New York, but
lived only a year after that uprooting, passing away in Auburn
on July 23, 1929. Her body was taken back to McConnelsville
where she was laid to rest amid the scenes that had endeared
themselves to her during her remarkably fruitful life of sixty-seven
years. She died in the spirit of some of her own stanzas, for in
her finest gospel song she had written,

"If you would join the glad songs of the blest, Let Jesus come into your heart;
If you would enter the mansions of rest, Let Jesus come into your heart."

Having fought the good fight about which she had sung at forty-three, and having found her Saviour "sweeter as the years go by" as she had sung at fifty, Lelia Naylor Morris entered into rest at the age of sixty-seven, in the assurance of the closing lines of her noblest hymn, in which she had sung,

4. Nearer, still nearer while life shall last; Till safe in glory my anchor is cast;
   Through endless ages, ever to be Nearer, my Saviour, still nearer to Thee.

123

16

SEPTIMUS WINNER

Whispering Hope

One of America's most versatile and successful poet-composers, Septimus Winner, was born in Philadelphia, Pennsylvania on May 11, 1827, the son of a violin maker, Joseph Eastburn Winner, and his wife, Mary Ann Hawthorne Winner. The lad's name was a prophecy of things to come rather than a numerical account of things already accomplished, for he did become the first of seven Winner children, the others being named in turn Julia, Margaret Ann, Sarah Jane, Joseph, Anna Ross and Sivori.

On his father's side, Septimus was descended from men of Revolutionary War fame, while he was related through his maternal grandfather, William Hawthorne, of New York City, to the renowned novelist Nathaniel Hawthorne. When the boy was thirteen, the family moved from the City of Brotherly Love to Wyoming Valley near Williamsport, Pennsylvania, where he attended the local school and worked for a while at the rural residence of Rev. Thomas P. Hunt. When his elementary classes were completed, Septimus returned to the city of his birth and entered the High School there, and it was in and around Philadelphia that the rest of his long, active and creative life was spent.

Learning the art of playing the violin from his father, Septimus soon mastered the instrument so well that by the time he was twenty years of age he went into the music teaching profession for himself, making a creditable business of teaching the violin, guitar and banjo. In fact, he did so well that on November 25, 1847, the twenty-year old instructor took as his bride Miss Hanna Jane Guyer, another Philadelphian, the ceremonies being solemnized by her pastor, Rev. Mr. Stork.

Although he began with a "bang", Septimus was soon experiencing the same financial ups and downs that had plagued his father during his younger years, and were to continue to haunt the elder Winner until his death in 1878 at the age of seventy-six. In 1848 the bride and bridegroom were living at 345 North Third Street, while the groom operated a music store and taught his pupils at 7 Arcade East. The very next year, however, he wrote in his diary, "I was thinking about the cost of building a house but came to my senses when I found I was too poor to pay for the digging of a foot of the cellar! What a state of affairs!"

Septimus and Hannah, like his own parents, had seven children born to their union, two of them dying in infancy, the names of the others being Emily Hawthorne, Ella Guyer, James Gibson, Mary Ann and Margaret Ferguson. It was in 1850 when the composer was in his twenty-third year, that he wrote and composed his first musical success, a sentimental song entitled "How Sweet Are The Roses", publishing it under a pseudonym taken in part from his mother's maiden name, Alice Hawthorne. In adopting a pen-name, Winner was merely following the custom of the day when Sidney Porter wrote under the name of O Henry, Samuel Clemens as Mark Twain, Henry Shaw as Josh Billings and Charles Browne as Artemus Ward. In future years, the name Alice Hawthorne was to conjure up memories of a dear sweet little old lady gowned in taffetta and lace and smelling of a sachet of crushed rose petals, but all the time the composer and poet behind the scenes was none other than Septimus Winner, the man who turned out more than twenty-three different successful music instruction books for as many as twenty-three different musical instruments, writing and composing dozens of popular songs as well as publishing piano and violin arrangements of nearly two-thousand other musical selections.

Winner soon followed up his first song success with a sequel, "My Cottage Home", and then turned out a tear-jerker that became all the rage in 1854, "What Is Home Without Mother?" That was the year, though, in which he really "hit his stride" and inscribed his name upon the scroll of musical immortals. In the early fall of 1854, Septimus, now twenty-seven years of age, heard a local colored boy, Dick Milburn, more familiarly known by his friends as "Whistling Dick", play his guitar and whistle and imitate the warble of a mocking bird. Winner was so taken with the lad's original interpretation that he was inspired to sit down and compose his most famous song, "Listen To The Mocking Bird", rewarding Dick by giving him a steady job in his music store! The three stanzas and chorus of Winner's outstanding success contained these lines:

1. I'm dreaming now of Hallie, sweet Hallie, sweet Hallie,
   I'm dreaming now of Hallie, For the thought of her is one that never dies;
   She's sleeping in the valley, the valley, the valley,
   She's sleeping in the valley, And the mocking bird is singing where she lies.

Chorus: Listen to the mocking bird, Listen to the mocking bird,
          The mocking bird still singing o'er her grave;
          Listen to the mocking bird, Listen to the mocking bird,
          Still singing where the weeping willows wave.

2. Ah! well, I yet remember, remember, remember,
   Ah! well, I yet remember, When we gathered in the cotton side by side;
   Twas in the mild September, September, September,
   Twas in the mild September, And the mocking bird was singing far and wide.

3. When the charms of spring awaken, awaken, awaken,
   When the charms of spring awaken, And the mocking bird is singing on the bough,
   I feel like one forsaken, forsaken, forsaken,
   I feel like one forsaken, Since my Hallie is no longer with me now.

Within half a century more than twenty-million copies of the song were sold, although poor Septimus had, with typical artistic lack of foresight, sold all of his rights to his publisher, Lee and Walker, for a paltry $5! On the wings of that song, thousands of baby girls all over the country were named "Hally" or "Hallie" the heroine over whose grave Septimus had the mocking bird mournfully singing.

His only other song that ever approached this one in popularity was a silly little chorus called "The Deutcher's Dog" in which a heart-broken old man sang in German dialect this mediocre bit of poetic doggerel to a melody about as "original" as the lyrics:

1. Oh, where, or where has my little dog gone? Oh where, oh where can he be?
   With his tail cut short and his ears cut long, Oh where, oh where can he be?

2. My little dog always waggles his tail Whenever he wants his grog;
   And if the tail were more strong than he, Why the tail would wag the dog!

The fact that this ditty was written to be sung in dialect gave rise to the claim that it was of German origin, when it was as American as Winner's "Mocking Bird".

While this masterpiece added little to the composer's coffers, it enhanced his fame and made his younger brother Joseph so jealous that he swore, in a moment of filial anger, that he could do as well, if not better. When challenged by Septimus to "put up or shut up", Joseph came through with a song as profound as the dialect ditty, an original composition all his very own about a "Little Brown Jug." Like his older brother, he hesitated to offer it for publication under his real name, so he took his father's middle name "Eastburn" as his pen-name, and it is as an "Eastburn" composition that this song lives on to this very day:

1. My wife and I lived all alone In a little log hut we called our own;
   She loved gin and I loved rum, I tell you what, we had lots of fun.

Chorus: Ha! ha! ha! You and me, Little Brown Jug don't I love thee!
   Ha! ha! ha! You and me, Little Brown Jug don't I love thee!

Six stanzas later Joseph's creative genius ran out, so he concluded his one claim to fame with this poetic apology:

6. The rose is red, my nose is too, The violet's blue and so are you;
   And yet I guess before I stop, I'd better take another drop!

In 1868, fourteen years after the "Mocking Bird", and possibly about the same time that the British artist George Frederic Watts (1817-1904) painted his most famous picture, "Hope", which portrayed a blind-folded maiden sitting atop the world, clutching in her left hand a lyre, all of whose strings but one had been broken, and in the tragic and soul-shattering "backwash" of the Civil War, forty-one year old Winner wrote his most popular and successful sacred song, the two stanzas and chorus of the perennial favorite "Whispering Hope", published under the name of Alice Hawthorne, and dedicated to Miss Dora C. Stiles of Stowe, Vermont. The reassuring words, penned to be sung to the poet's original flowing melody, are as follows:

1. Soft as the voice of an angel, Breathing a lesson unheard,
   Hope with a gentle persuasion Whispers her comforting word.
   Wait till the darkness is over, Wait till the tempest is done,
   Hope for the sunshine tomorrow, After the shower is gone.
Chorus: Whispering Hope, Oh, how welcome thy voice,
          Making my heart in its sorrow rejoice.
2. If in the dusk of the twilight Dim be the region afar,
   Will not the deepening darkness Brighten the glimmering star?
   Then when the night is upon us, Why should the heart sink away?
   When the dark midnight is over, Watch for the breaking of day.

In striking contrast to the spiritual mood of "Whispering Hope", is another spontaneous little song that Winner wrote on the spur of the moment at a children's party some time later, a song that children all over the country were soon singing enthusiastically:
One little, two little, three little Indians,
Four little, five little, six little Indians;
Seven little, eight little, nine little Indians; Ten little Indian boys.
Then, even before the days of the "capsule countdown", Winner had the children sing the song backwards, beginning with the "ten" and concluding with the "one".

In addition to sacred and secular songs on a wide variety of miscellaneous subjects, Winner tried his hand at patriotic poems and tunes during the dark, depressing days of the tragic Civil War, and came up with three, "The Arms Of Abraham", "Hoist Up The Flag", and the one that was the best of the three and the only one that caused him to clash with the politicians, "Give Us Back Our Old Commander". The incidents leading up to this tragic farce and Winner's arrest and threatened imprisonment as a "traitor" took place in this manner.

General George B. McClellan, a West Point graduate, was one of the Union's outstanding military men at the outbreak of the War of 1861-1865. In the first major battle of that four-year conflict, the Federals were defeated at the first battle of Manassas, or Bull Run, on July 21, 1861, by the Confederates under General Beauregard. It was during that struggle that southern General Bee cried, as he fell mortally wounded, "Rally around the Virginians. There stands Jackson like a stone-wall!" General McDowell had led the Federals in that disaster, when General Winfield Scott, Mexican war hero and Commander in Chief of the Union Armies, had been too ill to take an active part in the battle. When McDowell proved unsuccessful right from the start, Lincoln picked McClellan to head up his best army, since Little Mac had driven the enemy out of the western part of Virginia, the portion that later became a separate state, West Virginia, and was admitted to the Union in 1863. Mac's victory there had been greatly over-estimated and over-rated, since a large portion of the people there were already loyal and sympathetic with the Union cause. Anyway, at thirty-five, without extensive training or experience in the field, he was placed in supreme command by President Lincoln, since the Chief Executive could find no one else as capable for the job. Mac was an excellent trainer of troops, had a winning personality and was loved by all of his men, thousands of whom he knew by name. He assumed command in July 1861, after the catastrophe of First Manassas, but waited month after month to attack, until Lincoln became exasperated and ordered him to attack the enemy no later than February, 1862. The overall plan was for McClellan and McDowell to march by separate routes on Richmond, the Confederate capital, meeting on the outskirts of the Virginia city. Mac arrived within five miles of the city, coming up the Virginia peninsula between the James and York Rivers, advancing by way of Colonial Williamsburg. But McDowell's army never showed up and Mac hesitated to attack the city by himself. When General Lee took the field and raised the siege of Richmond, he forced McClellan back down the peninsula with tremendous losses, Mac finally succeeding in getting his men on boats at Harrison's Landing, and from there to the safety and security of nearby Fort Monroe in Hampton Roads. After those disasters, Lincoln removed McClellan from supreme command, but recalled him after the Second Battle of Manassas and the threatened invasion of Washington by the victorious Confederates under Generals Lee and Jackson. McClellan and Lee met at Antietam in September, 1862, where both sides suffered heavy losses, although the Union claimed the ultimate victory there. When McClellan failed to follow up his victory with the complete destruction of Lee's battered army, Lincoln became so enraged that once again he removed him from his top position, replacing him with General Burnside. In December 1862, Burnside suffered a tragic and costly defeat at Fredericksburg, where the Union forces tasted one of the worst defeats of the entire war. When thousands of soldiers deserted and hundreds of officers resigned in protest to the bungling leadership of General Burnside, the northern people began once again to call for General McClellan to lead their forces to victory, and to end the cruel and costly war then entering its third bloody year. Lincoln as well as the War Department opposed McClellan's reappointment on the ground that he was not aggressive enough and never attacked unless compelled to by the Commander In Chief. But to the people he was still a popular hero. When Septimus Winner visited Washington during those trying days and sensed the sentiment of the populace that demanded McClellan's reappointment, when he heard soldiers as well as civilians shout "Give us back Little Mac!" he returned to his Philadelphia home and, that very same evening, dashed off the stanzas and chorus of his new song "Give Us Back Our Old Commander, Little Mac, The People's Pride!" in which he sang:

1. Give us back our old Commander, Little Mac, the people's pride,
   Let the army and the nation In their choice be satisfied.
   With McClellan as our leader, Let us strike the blow anew,
   Give us back our old Commander, He will see the battle through.

Chorus: Give us back our old Commander, Let him manage, let him plan;

With McClellan as our leader, We can wish no better man.

Showing disdain for some of Lincoln's other appointees, Winner wrote:

3. Pope he made a dash for Dixie, Said he'd set the darkies free, But he hasn't done already What we did expect to see.

Down upon the Rappahannock, Burnside went with army bold;

Says he tried to do his duty, Acting not as he was told.

His sixth stanza poked scorn at President Lincoln and Secretary of War Stanton as well as at Generals Halleck and Fremont, just as stanza five had criticized politicians as well as newspaper editors like the renowned Horace Greely. Little wonder then that the poet-composer was "put on the carpet" for his supposedly "treasonable song".

Within a few days, more than eighty-thousand copies of this new song had been sold and it was being sung by nearly every soldier in the Army of the Potomac during their day's chores as well as around their nightly campfires. Secretary of War Stanton became so enraged over the song's theme and popularity that he called its singing "treason" and ordered the arrest and imprisonment of its composer, Septimus Winner, and then officially suppressed its use in the army, threatening with arrest any soldier heard singing any of its lines. Any actor on any stage anywhere caught doing the same thing was liable to the same punishment. Winner was actually brought before a military tribunal and charged with treason. He informed the tribunal and the Secretary of War that the song had been innocently composed without any thoughts of treason whatsoever! Still Stanton ordered all existing copies of the song destroyed and notified Winner that further publication of the song would result in his confinement at Fort Lafayette for the duration of the conflict! What a fate for the man who had written and composed "Whispering Hope"! When he promised to discontinue the sale of the song, Winner was released from custody. Thousands of copies of the new publication were thereupon destroyed and no more were subsequently published. But even Stanton could not stop the people from singing it, and sing it they did, openly defying Stanton's order. Meanwhile they continued to voice their approval of General McClellan. After Stanton's order, Julia Mortimer sang the new song in Washington's Ford Theatre (where Lincoln was later shot by Booth) without molestation or threat of arrest. Although the excitement eventually died down, Mac was never again restored to military power. He was nominated for President by the Democratic Party in 1864 but was defeated by Lincoln, by 2,330,552 to 1, 835,985 popular votes or 212 to 21 electoral votes. After Lincoln's assassination, the vice president Andrew Johnson became the chief executive, to be succeeded by Union General Ulysses Grant, who served two terms and then retired from the political arena, being followed in the high office by Rutherford B. Hayes. Hayes proved to be unpopular with the Republicans who wanted to give Grant a third term. Grant and his cohorts entered the convention that year with 306 pledged votes, a large bloc but not enough to defeat the opposing candidate James G. Blaine, or John Sherman who ran third. There was considerable opposition to giving Grant a third term, and on the thirty-sixth ballot James A. Garfield of Ohio became the party's official candidate, eventually winning the Presidency, only to be shot down a few months later by a disgruntled office seeker shortly after assuming office. During all the "ballyhoo" on Grant's behalf prior to Garfield's election, the friends and comrades of the former Union Commander in Chief picked up Winner's "treasonable" song, and applied it to their wartime hero, and began to sing "Give Us Back Our Old Commander". But even that move failed to rally sufficient support, although it did have quite an effect upon the delegates at the convention. Strangely enough, when applied to McClellan, Winner's song was criticized as "treason of the lowest order" but when applied to Grant several years later it was regarded as "patriotism of the highest order". Such are the fortunes of war and politics!

In his diary for 1902, under November 18, Winner wrote, "Went down to Catholic Church with Gib to hear them play 'Whispering Hope' in the evening." On November 22, 1902, he wrote, "A fine beautiful day, a nice parade with President

132

Roosevelt to open the new High School at Broad and Green." Little dreaming that that was to be the last day of his life, he had met in person, for the first time, a President, Theodore Roosevelt, and it was on that very same day, in his seventy-sixth year, that Septimus Winner died in the city of his birth, Philadelphia.

Wisely did a contemporary write of him, "He was one who deserves more of his countrymen than he is ever apt to receive," while another added, "In his songs and his poems he will live long after more ambitious celebrities have ceased to be remembered." Those who love and still sing "Whispering Hope" will unanimously concur!

* * * * *

133

17.

KNOWLES SHAW

Bringing In The Sheaves

Before he died, the humble Indiana farmer and tanner said of his son, the eldest of his three children, "Knowles is a puzzle to me; he will either make a terribly bad man or a very good one; whatever he does he will do it with all his might." The lad had been born to Albin and Huldah Shaw on October 13, 1834, while they were living in Butler County, Ohio, but they moved a few weeks after the birth of their first child to Rush County, Indiana, along with a group of other hard-working pioneers who sought a new life farther west.

When Knowles was just twelve years of age, his father took sick. Feeling that his end was near, Albin gave his eldest son one of his most prized possessions, a violin, and then followed that up with this fatherly admonition, "Be good to your mother and prepare to meet your God." Knowles felt the full weight of family responsibility when his father passed away a few days later, and he labored long and hard to help feed, clothe and house his mother and his two sisters during the next few years. In addition to working on the farm, he began to cultivate his gift of music, and soon was picking up more dollars playing the violin for community parties and dances than he could scrape up out of the rocky soil of the family farm. Neighbors said later that "Knowles Shaw's head was like a tar-bucket for everything that touched it stuck to it!"

Without formal education, he picked up learning everywhere he went, and soon was in demand as a musician and entertainer. It was then, in his late teens, that the second part of his father's dying advice struck him full in the heart and forced him to make his peace with God before he could find peace in his own soul.

Right in the middle of a big party, he suddenly realized that he had neglected the cultivation of his soul, so he put away his fiddle, prayed for forgiveness, attended the next Church service in nearby Flat Rock Church and received baptism on September 13, 1852. To the surprise of his friends, he never wavered in his determination to be a good Christian from that day on, but few dreamed that God had even larger fields of usefulness in store for the rawboned country boy. Step by step Knowles began to learn about the Christian life, but it was not until six years after his conversion that he opened his mouth in public "to say a good word for Jesus Christ". He always looked back upon that third Sunday in October, 1858, during his twenty-fourth year, the day when he actually spoke before a group of people on behalf of his Lord for the first time in his life, as one of the most memorable days he was ever privileged to live.

By that time, however, he had married Martha Finley on January 11, 1855, and had been blessed with the birth of a daughter, Georgie, on June 3, 1856, while the birth of Mary Elizabeth occurred on October 31, 1858, just a few days after Knowles' first public address. Full grown by now, he stood six feet and four inches tall, commanding attention by his height as well as by his musical skill and voice. The year 1859 saw him conducting his first series of revival services, and by 1861, two years later, he was being widely heralded as "the singing evangelist" of Indiana, and invitations were coming in from nearby towns and cities for more and more series of revival meetings. For the next thirteen years, Knowles Shaw travelled the length and breadth of the country, preaching in city after city and state after state, never in that entire time being without a preaching appointment for two weeks in succession.

Meantime, three other children were born to Knowles and Martha, their presence in the home softening the blow which came with the passing of the last two in their infancy, and the death of their eldest daughter, Georgie, during her fourteenth year. This tragedy inspired Shaw to write a simple gospel song which he entitled "Lambs Of The Upper Fold", in which he spoke of his departed children as "tender lambs" in Jesus' keeping. Soon Knowles was not only preaching the gospel but singing it as well, several contemporaries comparing his voice to that of Ira D. Sankey and Philip Bliss in its power to move and melt the hearts of his hearers. The songbooks that he published contained many of his own original stanzas and tunes, one or two of which became quite popular, but it was his preaching that attracted the multitudes, for in it, one listener said, "he reasoned like Paul, was as bold as Peter and as tender as John, as natural as Shakespeare, witty as Swift, pathetic as Burns, independent as Beecher, idiosyncratic as Talmadge, and indefatigable as Dwight L. Moody," a rare combination indeed for any evangelist, past, present or future!

When he prepared a sermon on "The Handwriting On The Wall" on one occasion, he thought of his own past life and the marvelous way God had directed him out of the paths of sin into the paths of righteousness, and was immediately inspired to write a new hymn, putting the content of his message into the new stanzas. Taking the story directly out of the fifth chapter of Daniel in The Old Testament, in which the Hebrew prophet interpreted for the Babylonian King Belshazzar the meaning of the mysterious words which a hand had written on the wall during the King's feast, "Mene, Mene, Tekel, Upharsin", Shaw wrote his stanzas as follows:

1. At the feast of Belshazzar and a thousand of his lords,
   While they drank from golden vessels as the Book of Truth records —
   In the night as they revelled in the royal palace hall,
   They were seized with consternation — twas a Hand upon the wall!

Chorus: Tis the hand of God on the wall! Tis the hand of God on the wall!
   Shall the record be "Found wanting!" or shall it be "Found trusting!"
   While that hand is writing on the wall?

2. See the brave captive, Daniel, as he stood before the throng,
   And rebuked the haughty monarch for his mighty deeds of wrong;
   As he read out the writing, twas the doom of one and all,
   For the kingdom now was finished, said the Hand upon the wall!

3. See the faith, zeal and courage that would dare to do the right,
   Which the Spirit gave to Daniel — twas the secret of his might,
   In his home in Judaea or a captive in the hall,
   He understood the writing of his God upon the wall!
4. So our deeds are recorded, there's a Hand that's writing now;
   Sinner, give your heart to Jesus, to His royal mandates bow;
   For the day is approaching, it must come to one and all,
   When the sinner's condemnation will be written on the wall!

Shaw set his own stanzas to a melody that was later arranged by composer E. O. Excell, and the new song was sung as a sacred solo with dramatic effect by none other than Ira D. Sankey himself, and included in his collection "Gospel Hymns, Numbers 1 to 6, Complete".

Shaw's most popular gospel song, and the one that has outlived "The Handwriting On The Wall" was written as a poetic tribute to a dear preacher friend, A. D. Fillmore, who, like Shaw himself, had been a minister, evangelist, singer, composer and gospel song writer, and whose publication "The Christian Psalmist" in 1847 was to go into eighteen different editions during the next century, and whose son, Charles Fillmore, was to write the popular gospel song of the next generation, "Tell Mother I'll Be There", in 1896. As Knowles Shaw thought of the way that Rev. Mr. Fillmore had brought in such a marvelous harvest of souls during the years of his active ministry, he was inspired to sit down and pen several original stanzas, whose principle theme was taken in part from Psalm 126: 5-6, "They that sow in tears shall reap in joy. He that goeth forth and weepeth bearing precious seed, shall doubtless come again with rejoicing, bringing his sheaves with him." As the preacher-poet pictured his co-worker "bringing in his sheaves", he wrote these descriptive stanzas:

1. Sowing in the morning, sowing seeds of kindness,
   Sowing in the noontide and the dewy eve.
   Waiting for the harvest and the time of reaping,
   We shall come rejoicing, bringing in the sheaves.
2. Sowing in the sunshine, sowing in the shadows,
   Fearing neither clouds nor winter's chilling breeze;

By and by the harvest and the labor ended,
We shall come rejoicing, bringing in the sheaves.
3. Going forth with weeping, sowing for the Master,
Though the loss sustained our spirit often grieves;
When our weeping's over, He will bid us welcome,
We shall come rejoicing, bringing in the sheaves.

When George A. Minor set those stanzas to music, he made a Chorus in the style of the day by repeating the theme "Bringing in the sheaves" several times, along with the last line of the first stanza, and Shaw's new gospel song began to sing its way around the Christian world. Carrying out his own admonition, Shaw in the fifteen years of his public ministry received more than eleven thousand people into the fellowship of the Church. At the height of his influence, and just four months prior to his forty-fourth birthday, Knowles Shaw concluded a five-week series of evangelistic meetings at the Commerce Street Christian Church in Dallas, Texas, and boarded the Houston and Central Texas Railroad Train on June 7, 1878, to join his family in their Columbus, Mississippi, home. However, a disastrous accident prevented that reunion from taking place. Twenty-seven passengers were injured when the train left the track two miles south of McKinney station at quarter past nine that night, but there was just one fatality, Rev. Knowles Shaw. The evangelist was caught in the wreckage and despite the frantic efforts of his friends and travelling companions to extricate him, he died before portions of the car could be cut away. His last words were, "O it is a grand thing to rally people to the cross of Christ." Thus passed this unusual and remarkable man in the prime of his life and at the height of his powers. The finest tribute his friends paid him at his funeral service as well as at countless memorial services that were held throughout the country was this: "He not only wrote 'Bringing In The Sheaves', he actually went out into the Lord's harvest fields and brought thousands of them in with his own hands, to present them to the Lord of the harvest and to hear His words, 'Well done, good and faithful servant; enter thou into the joy of thy Lord'."

18.

WILLIAM O. CUSHING

Follow On   Jewels
Ring The Bells Of Heaven   Under His Wings

According to one biographer, Rev. William Orcutt Cushing (1823-1902) was forced to surrender his pulpit when he suddenly lost his power of speech. Like Samson without his hair, Cushing knew that without his voice, his usefulness as a Christian minister was at an end. A native of Hingham, Massachusetts, where he had been born on the last day of 1823, the clergyman had early offered himself for full-time Christian service and had prepared for the ministry and been ordained as a preacher, only to have his usefulness tragically terminated when he learned that he had lost his power of speech. Despite that tragedy, Cushing still felt in his heart that God had called him to some specific task which would redound to His glory, and that, in His own good time, He would open another door of usefulness to him, once the door of preaching had been closed. In that spirit of acceptance and faith, he knelt and prayed, "O Lord, give me something to do for Thee!" whereupon God answered his earnest prayer and gave to him the gift of writing hymns and sacred songs, a talent which he never knew he possessed but the one by means of which his influence continues to be a vital one to this very day. Possibly that gift had always been with him, but it took a disappointment to uncover or reveal it to the poet himself as well as to the outside world.

While many of his fellow clergymen were preaching sermons on the familiar words of the Psalmist, "I will lift up mine eyes unto the hills from whence cometh my help," Cushing was wondering when he would hear a sermon on "How To Find God In Life's Valleys". The Shepherd King had written in Psalm

139

Twenty-Three, "Yea, though I walk through the valley of the shadow of death, I will fear no evil for Thou art with me" and it was that particular verse rather than the one about the God of the mountains that sustained the heart-broken minister during his months of re-adjustment. Emerging out of his own personal "valley of sorrow" undiscouraged and determined to serve God and make his "life count for Jesus", the preacher-poet began to write himself into immortality, reaching a vaster audience with his pen than he would ever have been privileged to touch from a pulpit. Reflecting upon this experience in 1878, when he was fifty-five years of age, as he passed through another spiritual crisis during which he had a deep longing to give his all for Christ Who had given His life for him, Cushing was inspired to write a gospel song that was about as autobiographical as a song-poem could be. He called his hymn simply "Follow On" and later confessed that "it was written with prayer and the hope that some heart might by it be led to give up all for Christ." His three stanzas contained these lines:

1. Down in the valley with my Saviour I would go,
   Where the flowers are blooming and the sweet waters flow;
   Everywhere He leads me I would follow, follow on,
   Walking in His footsteps till the crown be won.

Chorus: Follow, follow, I would follow Jesus; Anywhere, everywhere, I would follow on;
   Follow, follow, I would follow Jesus, Everywhere He leads me I would follow on.

2. Down in the valley with my Saviour I would go,
   Where the storms are beating and the dark waters flow;
   With His hand to lead me I will never, never fear;
   Danger cannot fright me if my Lord is near.

3. Down in the valley or upon the mountain steep,
   Close beside my Saviour would my soul ever keep;
   He will lead me safely in the paths that He has trod,
   Up to where they gather on the hills of God.

Two years later the well-known Baptist clergyman, college professor, poet and composer, Rev. Robert Lowry (1826-1899) discovered Cushing's stanzas and immediately set them to music as he had so successfully composed tunes for "Something For

Thee", "Christ Arose", "All The Way My Saviour Leads Me", "Shall We Gather At The River" and other familiar hymns and sacred songs. The poet himself admitted that "much of the power and usefulness of the hymn are due to Mr. Lowry who put it into song." It was received so enthusiastically that its copyright was renewed in 1908 by the composer's widow, since the original copyright, taken out in 1880, had expired at the end of twenty-eight years.

Strangely enough, Cushing was not the only Christian poet to versify this idea. C. Austin Miles, author-composer of "In The Garden" in 1912, had written along similar lines when, in 1908, at the age of forty, he had written the words and music of the gospel song, "If Jesus Goes With Me", which began:

1. "It may be in the valley where countless dangers hide;
   It may be in the sunshine that I, in peace, abide;
   But this one thing I know, if it be dark or fair,
   If Jesus goes with me, I'll go anywhere."

Chorus: "If Jesus goes with me I'll go, anywhere!
   Tis heaven to me, where'er I may be, if He is there!
   I count it a privilege here His cross to bear;
   If Jesus goes with me I'll go, anywhere!"

In the life of every Christian there are as many "ups" as "downs" and as many "dark nights of the soul" as "bright sunshiny days" when he catches a glimpse of glory through some rifted cloud atop some lofty peak, far removed from the mundane pressures of everyday living. And soon after his time of trial, testing and re-dedication, Cushing, in 1856, at the age of thirty-three, was inspired to write what was to become one of the finest children's hymns in all Christian literature, "Jewels", later set to lilting music by George F. Root (1820-1895) the prolific author and composer of the most popular patriotic and sentimental songs of the Civil War era, as well as the composer of some splendid hymn tunes:

1. When He cometh, when He cometh To make up His jewels;
   All His jewels, precious jewels, His loved and His own:

Chorus: Like the stars of the morning His bright crown adorning,
   They shall shine in their beauty, Bright gems for His crown.

2. He will gather, He will gather The gems for His kingdom;
   All the pure ones, all the bright ones, His loved and His own.
3. Little children, little children, Who love their Redeemer,
   Are the jewels, precious jewels, His loved and His own.

A poem that Ira D. Sankey set to music proved to be another of Cushing's earlier successes, and was included in the composer's collection, "Gospel Hymns Complete, Numbers One to Six" in 1894, bearing the title "Hiding In Thee" and containing these lines suggested by and somewhat reminiscent of Augustus Montague Toplady's majestic hymn "Rock Of Ages":

1. O safe to the Rock that is higher than I,
   My soul in its conflicts and sorrows would fly;
   So sinful, so weary, Thine, Thine would I be;
   Thou blest "Rock Of Ages", I'm hiding in Thee.
2. In the calm of the noontide, in sorrow's lone hour,
   In times when temptation casts o'er me its power;
   In the tempest of life, on its wide heaving sea,
   Thou blest "Rock Of Ages", I'm hiding in Thee.
3. How oft in the conflict, when pressed by the foe,
   I have fled to my Refuge, and breathed out my woe;
   How often when trials, like sea-billows, roll,
   Have I hidden in Thee, O Thou Rock of my soul.

The phrase in Psalm 61:2, "When my heart is overwhelmed, lead me to the rock that is higher than I", had caught Cushing's fancy as it had that of Erastus Johnson, inspiring him to pen the stanzas of his finest gospel song, "The Rock That Is Higher Than I".

When Cushing heard a secular song, "The Little Octoroon", which George F. Root had written and composed, the music so intrigued him that he could not get it out of his mind. "The melody ran in my head all day long," he wrote, "chiming and flowing in its sweet musical cadence. I wished greatly that I might secure the tune for use in the Sunday School and for other Christian purposes. When I heard the bells of heaven ringing over some sinner that had returned, it seemed like a glad day. Then the words 'Ring The Bells Of Heaven' at once flowed down into the waiting melody" and thus did one of the finest Root-Cushing gospel songs come into existence:

1. Ring the bells of heaven, there is joy today, For a soul returning from the wild;
   See the Father meets him out upon the way, Welcoming His
   weary, wandering child.
Chorus: Glory, glory, how the angels sing; Glory, glory, how the
   loud harps ring;
   Tis the ransomed army, like a mighty sea, Pealing forth
   the anthem of the free.

It was later in his long life that the former preacher returned
to the basic theme of one of his earlier efforts, and undertook to
improve upon those initial lines and phrases, producing another
poem that Sankey was also to set to music and describe as "among
my later compositions". Although Cushing was familiar with
such Biblical phrases as David's cry in Psalm 55:6, "Oh that I
had the wings of a dove, then I would fly away and be at rest,"
and the major Old Testament prophet's statement in Isaiah
40:31, "they shall mount up with wings as eagles," he was more
deeply impressed with the fact that the Psalmist and the Prophet
alike testified to the safety and security they figuratively and poeti-
cally found "under the shadow of His wings." Jesus Himself, the
preacher recalled, had longed to gather His own people in His
sheltering arms as a hen gathers her chicks under her wings, but
they would not come to Him nor permit Him to protect them in
that manner. Moved by such words as Psalm 17:8, "Hide me
under the shadow of thy wings", Psalm 61:4, "I will trust in
the covert of thy wings", and Psalm 91:4, "under His wings shalt
thou trust", the Massachusetts minister out of his own experiences,
penned one of his finest hymns, copyrighted in 1896, the year of
its composition:

1. Under His wings I am safely abiding, Though the night
   deepens and tempests are wild;
   Still I can trust Him; I know He will keep me; He has redeemed me and I am His child.
Chorus: Under His wings, Under His wings; Who from His
   love can sever?
   Under His wings my soul shall abide, Safely abide forever.

2. Under His wings, what a refuge in sorrow! How the heart
   yearningly turns to His rest!
   Often when earth has no balm for my healing, There I find
   comfort and there I am blest.
3. Under His wings, Oh what precious enjoyment! There will
   I hide till life's trials are o'er;
   Sheltered, protected, no evil can harm me; Resting in Jesus,
   I'm safe evermore.

Soon this new hymn became so popular that the students at
Dwight L. Moody's Northfield, Massachusetts, school sang it as
their leader entered the seminary building for morning worship
each day.

From the day he wrote "Jewels" as a young man of thirty-three
in 1856, until he penned "Under His Wings" as a mature Christian of seventy-three in 1896, Rev. W. O. Cushing wrote his
songs of hope and heaven, love and laughter, faith and fortitude,
promise and perseverance, and prior to his death at the age of
seventy-nine on October 19, 1902, he had the satisfaction of
knowing that although he could not speak with his audible voice,
God had placed a pen in his hand and a song in his heart, by
means of which he had set Christendom to singing.

Index of Hymns And Sacred Songs
(Numbers refer to Chapters)

Index Of Songs
(Numbers refer to Chapters)

Index Of People
(Numbers refer to Chapters)